YOU MIGHT
BE AN
OVERWEIGHT
AMERICAN
IF...

Library of Congress Control Number:

ISBN: 979-8-234-04398-6

YOU MIGHT BE AN OVERWEIGHT AMERICAN IF...

★ ★ ★

An Original Collection of

Hilarious Satirical Sketches and Monologues,

One-Liners, Stand-Up Comedy and Wiseass Wit

PAUL DOODY

CONTENTS

1

LAMAZE COACHING FOR
HOT DOG EATING CONTEST
BREATHING TECHNIQUES

YOU JUST KNOW your wife is probably going to spoil the solemnity of your final words on your death bed by interrupting and saying "Honey? I realize this might not be a good time to remind you of this, but, if I've told you once I've told you a thousand times, it's really not polite to talk with food in your mouth."

When your wife makes a huge meal for dinner, you always know when you've finally had enough when you hear her yell "breakfast is ready".

When people ask you "Do you know the time?" and you take a quick glance at your watch, it's not helpful when you tell them "Thanks for reminding me. It looks like it's just about time for a snack".

You wish you had a nickel for every time a complete stranger used the icebreaker on you of "I'll bet it would be one heck of a challenge for a guy as fat as you to remember the last time you ever did anything on an empty stomach."

One of the greatest loves of your life is hot dogs, but you vowed to never even touch one again. As much as you've tried to forget, every time you tried to eat one before you quit forever just brought back harrowing memories of coming in an embarrassing 2nd place for the first time ever at your last hot dog eating contest.

Restaurant dishwashers love when you're in the restaurant during their shift when they notice all of the plates and utensils the busboys drop off have been licked clean. Somehow they know they have you to thank for helping them out on their job.

You're the type of boss who tries to encourage employees to talk by telling them "There are no dumb questions". You stopped saying that though because every time you did, you'd hear a lot of snickering after some wise guy replied "Oh No? What about when Burger King asks you 'would you like to super-size your order?'".

Whenever old friends hear from you on July 4th, you act like you're just catching up on the old times making small talk, but they know by now that you just called to brag about medaling in the Nathan's hot dog eating contest again.

You think it's so eerie when you suspect friends can actually read your mind when they tell you "Now that dinner is over, I'll bet there's a 10 to 1 chance you're probably already wondering what you're going to eat next."

As you're eating at a restaurant, you wonder why people are always sneaking peeks at what you've eaten and then give you disgusted looks. It's obvious to you that they clearly think it's disgusting how much you ate for dinner. That's what's so comical about this. In your mind, you just started thinking about what you'd like for dinner after you just finished off the last of the appetizers.

When people look at all your empty plates and bowls at a restaurant, they naturally assume all the other contestants who lost must have left and you're just waiting for your prize after winning whatever legendary eating contest it was that just ended.

When co-workers at a company 'meet and greet' are uncomfortable about what to say to someone as fat as you without offending you, the icebreaker they usually decide on to start a conversation is "Soooo… have you broken any personal eating records lately?" It's happened so often at these socials, you just dread when it's like you can mouth the words for them the next time someone is about to ask. If that wasn't bad enough, the worst part of this harassment is that it still works like a charm on you as you start chattering like a school girl about all your recent eating contest heroics.

All the pregnant mothers were surprised to learn you were only in their Lamaze class to learn better eating contest breathing techniques.

You attend hot dog eating contests all over the country to learn the techniques of the champions because you can never seem to get enough to eat at work during your 30-minute lunch break.

Too many times to count, you've made stupid people curious enough that they feel compelled to ask you "I'm not sure I heard you correctly. Did I just hear you say you're busy planning a boring day? Why in the world would you do something like that?". At irritating moments like this, you almost want to say something mean and sarcastic to someone who clearly knows nothing about the lives of fat people. You always take it easy on them instead though and say "Well duhhh, silly…You must not know too many fat people. We're always able to eat a lot more than normal when we're bored".

You love your job and one of the 'all-time great' careers you've had, but announced you were retiring at the end of the season because the traveling was killing you and you wanted to spend more time with your family. Your loyal fans understood, but were stunned and heartbroken all the same when it seemed like you were just reaching your prime. As a tribute to recognize all your amazing records that will never be broken, the league commissioner waived the normal 7 year waiting period and immediately inducted you into the Hot Dog Eating Contest Hall of Fame.

Your wife knows better now that there's no logical need to ever ask you "Are you full yet?" anymore. She now understands why you always used to sound irritated when you told her sarcastically "Uhhhh…duhhh…does it look like I'm full yet?". She has no idea how she missed the obvious clue the first time, but knows now she can look and tell for herself that you're finally full when French fries start coming out of your nose and ears.

Whenever you pass out while you're eating at your favorite buffet, secret admirer waiters have always been able to revive you by whispering in your ear "Come on lardbutt, you're only 2 burgers away from breaking the all-time burger bar record. You've gotta' pull it together before the EMT's get here! YOU MAY NEVER HAVE THIS CHANCE AGAIN!!!"

All your favorite stories, which everyone has heard five times before, end with you saying with a look of utter disbelief "To this day, I still can't believe I ate the whole thing".

You're known as "a man of few words" but it's only because your mother taught you that it's not polite to speak with your mouth full.

When you gained fame as a hot dog eating contest champion, the best-seller for contest merchandise sales was a bobble head of you with a bobble body.

You were amazed when the judges somehow declared you the unofficial winner at a national hot dog eating contest. At the time, you were just minding your own business while you were having your normal afternoon snack in the fan section. As they were about to announce the contest winner though, who'd eaten 50 hot dogs, someone noticed you had over 60 hot dog wrappers at your feet.

Neighbors think you have a strobe light in the kitchen but it's actually from the refrigerator door opening and closing so often all night.

It's discouraging to know there's a high probability that your family won't be able to make out your solemn last words when you utter them. The reason is, based on their previous observations, there's about a 90% chance you'll be talking with your mouth full at the time.

You know that to everyone else in the restaurant you always look like you couldn't eat another bite before you even start eating. That's why you explain to your weight therapist that even when you're not that hungry you feel insulted and always end up eating like you've got to prove everyone wrong for not believing in you.

A lot of people assume you've taken some kind of vow of silence because they've never heard you talk before. The real reason is much simpler: you were taught it's bad manners to talk when your mouth is full.

You can always tell when McDonald's is having one of those big 2 for the price of 1 Big Mac promotions. At any given time during these deals there's at least 10 to 12 Chevette compacts parked just beyond the drive thru window. When you take a closer look, you'll notice an enormous American sitting in each car with an "Ohh shit! What have I gone and done now?!?" expression who all look a lot like a python that just swallowed a hippopotamus. This can only mean one thing: they even surprised themselves how much they ate and now realize they have to sit and digest for a couple of hours because there isn't a chance in hell they'll be able to steer the car until their bellies recede a couple of feet.

You couldn't possibly stuff even one more hot dog in after you won the county fair hot dog eating contest. That's why you decided to enter the pie eating contest instead of boiled egg eating afterwards because you've always been able to find room for dessert even when you're stuffed.

The last time one of your so-called friends offended your honor, you immediately stood up to him by challenging this cocky bastard to a pie eating duel to the death, only to watch him run off like the coward he is.

Understandably, you assumed your parents didn't like talking to you when you were a kid because any time you started to say something important to them, they would always tell you "Please don't talk with your mouth full."

Even though you've met a lot of dumb people in your life, no one's ever been dumb enough yet to ask you "Have you had enough to eat yet?"

Your wife has always tried to find ways to get your eating under control. One time she even had the hare-brained scheme to set a 10-minute time limit for you to eat all you could eat before she stopped serving you. That's why, during your acceptance speech into the Nathan's Hot Dog Eating Hall of Fame, you got teary-eyed and said "I owe it all to you honey for providing me the motivation to become the legendary champion I am today."

On the rare occasions you're not eating, one of your favorite pastimes is to sit around and chew the fat.

You've studied python eating habits because sometimes, when there's still food on your plate and your jaw is just too tired to chew anymore, you wanted to see if you could learn to finish the leftovers by swallowing them whole.

Sometimes after you've pigged out and you just know you couldn't take another bite, you end up just swallow-ing what's left.

I think I'm becoming a lot more philosophical about my overeating habits these days. The other day I went to a chili buffet for the day and when I went to bed that night, I had the mind-blowing thought "If I fart in bed, but my wife wasn't there to hear it, would it still make a noise?"

Sometimes when you try to be polite and tell someone "I couldn't eat another bite", they convince you to by giving a disappointed look and telling you "You can't be serious? There's no way you can stop now. Just try to imagine that this next bite is going to shatter the world record. You can do it!!!"

If there's edible road kill on your way to work, you'll make sure there's none on your way home.

When you look at people like they're idiots when they ask you "So...what do you do in your free time?", you tell them "Well duhhhh... doesn't it look like I like to do things that are fattening? After I'm finished doing that

- and that could be awhile - I like to sit down, relax and think about what I'm going to eat next".

You were disgusted when you finally entered the July 4th Nathan's Famous 10-minute hot dog eating contest because, even though you broke their pathetic contest record, you couldn't set a personal best because they ran out of hot dogs with 5 minutes to go.

Whenever you've been silent for a while at a work meeting and then look like you have something important to say, it never fails that when you say "I've been doing a lot of thinking lately..." some wise guy always interrupts by saying "Wait a minute! I'll bet I know what you're thinking: you've finally decided and now you're going to announce what you plan to eat next?"

Most of the talking you do now involves ordering your food at a drive thru. Otherwise, you usually tell people who call you "Look, I'm really too busy chewing and swallowing to talk right now. I'll get back to you in a couple of days when I'm done."

When you're surprisingly not chewing or swallowing now, it's very likely because you're probably waiting for your food to arrive.

Every meal at your house looks like the closing seconds of a 'neck and neck' finish of the annual Nathan's hot dog Eating World Championship.

Everything on your bucket list involves eating a bucket of it before you die.

Most of your personal goals concern how many of something you can eat in 10 minutes.

You think the dumbest question anyone ever asked you was "Did you get enough to eat?"

My wife hates when we don't make a dinner reservation at a restaurant and then discovers when we get there that there's a long wait to be seated. She does enjoy the part where she gets to sit at the bar after a tough work week and have some leisurely time to relax and have a few drinks before we eat. What embarrasses her to no end though is, while she's enjoying herself at the bar, I prefer to hang out at the exit making appetizer offers to customers who are leaving by saying "Psssttt... Heh, buddy, I'll give you $20 bucks for whatever you've got in that doggy bag".

You know fat people must definitely start pigging out the moment they leave the fast food drive thru yet, oddly enough, you never hear news reports about them choking to death behind the wheel. A recent medical journal article on innovative Heimlich maneuver techniques from the Extra Mayo Clinic has resolved this mystery, which also explains why so many fat guys drive Smart cars. It turns out that when a fat guy's belly is plastered against the steering wheel, it's an ideal situation to utilize a self-Heimlich technique simply by slamming your brake pedal to the floor so the belly recoil will dislodge whatever you're choking on at the time. I wish I had known about this method sooner, but at least it explains why I've had 5 life-saving, intentional rear-end accidents leaving McDonalds drive thru's in the last 6 months.

When I was a chubby kid, my mother always told me I had to wait at least one hour before I could go back in the pool, yet I could go right back in the water after I finished eating when we were at the beach. In our house, this rule wasn't about advice for cramps. She just wanted to make sure I could fit back in the pool without getting stuck.

You're so ashamed of your weight, it makes you scared to death of dying from overeating and having everyone ridicule you when they read your obituary and the cause says you ate yourself to death. That's why you've taken up bungee jumping and exposing yourself to more 2nd hand smoke lately. If you die prematurely now, noth-ing would please you more than preserving the family's honor with a death notice that read "Man smoking a cigarette and eating a Double Whopper dies in tragic bungee jumping accident when the allegedly 'defective' cord failed to recoil. Although preliminary, the county coroner believes 2nd hand smoke may have triggered this tragic accident."

As soon as you finish eating, your ferocious, wild-eyed, shark feeding frenzy expression disappears and is replaced by a fragile and frantic "I wonder what I should eat next?" expression.

Your wife knows better now than to ever tell you "You shouldn't be snacking so much before dinner. I made a big meal and you're going to ruin your appetite." She now knows that laying down the gauntlet like that only motivates you to think "I'll show her a thing or two about trying to ruin my appetite!". After setting a new personal record for pigging out on pre-dinner snacks, out of pure spite, you set another record-breaking dinner eating per-formance immediately afterwards for Taco Tuesday.

Whenever people seem fascinated with you they always seem to want to hear more about all your personal best eating records.

One of your favorite things you like to do on lazy Saturday afternoons is watch competitive eating compe-titions from home and easily match the declared winner hot dog for hot dog before your wife yells "Stop eating those hot dog appetizers. Dinner is ready."

You keep a survival Road Kill recipe book in your car trunk with a Hibachi grill in case you're ever stuck in a traffic jam again for more than 30 minutes.

You made an appointment when you figured you must have sleep apnea because you wake up so tired all the time. Your doctor shocked you though when he told you your only problem is that you're having trouble breathing between bites when you eat in your sleep.

Whenever anyone's ever asked you "Do you think you'll have enough time to eat?" 5 minutes later, after you got up from laughing on the floor, you've always answered "Well, duhhhh. That's funny, but doesn't it look like I'd need to find the time to eat anyway even if I didn't?"

You used to be a "seeing is believing" type when you were young and inexperienced. As you aged and gained weight though, you broadened your perspective and became more of a "the proof is in the 6 bowls of pudding" type.

After any strenuous competition you've always enjoyed sitting down afterwards to have a relaxing meal to reward your effort. That's why some of the TV reporters were shocked after they asked you how you planned to celebrate after setting a world record in the July 4th hot dog eating contest and you told them "I'm going to the Golden Corral!".

You never can please a wife. When the honeymoon was over, my wife announced her first married pet peeve about me and asked "If it's not too big of a sacrifice for you, can you not speak with your mouth full all the time? It's sooo disgusting when fat people do that." I didn't think that was too oppressive of a post-honeymoon, marriage commitment so I willingly obliged. Not a week later though, she started nagging "You've grown distant already since our honeymoon ended. You haven't said more than 2 words to me all week. Don't you love me anymore?" Caught off guard in what was clearly an important relationship defining moment, all I could think to do was scribble a quick note that said "Don't talk crazy, honey. Of course I still love you. I can explain everything, but please give me a minute to finish chewing and swallowing so I don't break your Rule #1 and speak with my mouth full."

You're nothing like the usual type of timid, overweight guys who are embarrassed about their weight in public and avoid all forms of confrontation to avoid humiliating, public ridicule. You're proud to be an overweight American, where at least you know you're free… to eat anything. Your belief is you are the epitome of the modern American adaptation of the 'Land of the free and home of the brave' rugged individualists who built this country and didn't take any shit from anyone. Unlike lovable, cuddly fat guys, you believe it's better to be feared than loved and conduct yourself with an 'If it's in your way, eat it' indomitable spirit that makes anyone in your path tremble with fear. Some of the worst hecklers who normally torment someone like you into submission with their ridicule are quiet as a church mice when you pass. They know that any insult to your honor in the past has always led to a duel to the death hot dog eating contest, which always humbles arugula salad eating, health food sissies into silence.

2

THE REVISED AMERICAN KARMA SUTRA GUIDE FOR SUFFOCATION AVOIDANCE TECHNIQUES DURING SEX

ONE OF THE most amazing aspects about American lifestyles these days is it's not hard at all for a 500-pound bully to go find a fight when you tell him "Why don't you go pick on someone your own size?"

Before the Big Mac was invented, in the history of humanity no one had ever seen a drive thru lane butt cheek neck brace until you pulled up one day and ordered 8 Big Macs.

You watch the Biggest Loser show, but it's only so you can find the contact information for contestants so you can make a lowball bid on their snack closet leftovers and 'One size fits all' Snuggie wardrobe.

You've played the American version of Russian roulette when the refrigerator is empty by seeing if you can eat the cheese from the mousetraps before they snap.

The Domino's delivery driver wasn't able to get a restraining order to keep you at a safe distance from him, but did get one that requires you to stay at least 500 feet away from his pizzas.

The best thing fat guys have going for them in this increasingly obese, American society is more and more men's clothing stores are finally caving in to the growing customer outcry and adding male maternity clothes departments to replace their discriminatory, fat-shaming 'one size fits all' leisure wear.

Americans used to be fascinated with the variety of sex positions in the ancient Karma Sutra guide. Now that most of the country is extra-chunky though, the new best seller in America on the subject of sex is from another ancient scroll called "Sex Techniques for Sumo Wrestlers".

It must be hard being gay in America, but it's got to be even harder when you're really fat. Can you imagine not being able to come out of the closet when you're finally ready to let the whole world know just because you couldn't fit in there in the first place?

You replaced your old coffee table with one more appropriate for your dining habits called a Coffee & Doughnuts table for the modern, overweight American. The design is similar, but instead of the standard two by four-foot coffee table, this one is 20 x 40 feet to provide enough extra room for the doughnuts.

You filed a lawsuit for discrimination after McDonald's hired you when they changed the sign on the bathroom mirror to 'Employees must wash hands AND be able to wipe their own butt before returning to work'.

You lost your lawsuit against NASCAR because even though you were the inventor of the head and neck safety brace for crashes, the one they use isn't made out of enormous butt cheeks.

The yoga pants fad has become an epidemic in America for women. What's strange about that is, at most, only 2% of all American women look amazingly sexy in them. For the other 98%, there seems to be no logical reason you can think of for them to be parading their enormous butts in public. My guess is that the 98%'ers must think someone is going to get a major cash award from Lululemon one of these days for setting the elasticity record for how much ass they can stuff into one pair of yoga pants on the Faces of Walmart.

True love in an American marriage is demonstrated by intentionally gaining more weight than your wife does on your fad diet before you both quit that gimmicky scam of a diet.

You can bet your life on it that any American woman who has more than 20 diet and exercise books on her book shelf hasn't lost a pound in 20 years.

As a game show contestant one time, the host asked you to tell him something fascinating about yourself. You told him "Well Bob, you're not going to believe this, but I can make butt dials on anyone's phone within 10 feet of me with just a flick of a butt cheek…Sounds hard to believe, huh? Well, do you hear the ringing on the phone in your pocket? I just called Domino's to have a pizza delivered."

When you're blocking an entire aisle at Walmart and tell other shoppers "I'm sorry. Let me suck in my gut so you can try to squeeze by.", they usually ask you "Would you mind if I climbed over instead? No offense, but that defi-nitely looks like it would be the shorter way".

By the looks of about 80% of the shoppers at any mall in America, you would think business should be booming in the U.S. for the confidential purchase of bidet toilets for customers whose arms don't reach around far enough anymore to be able to wipe their own butt.

Except for the constant noise from chomping, gulping, swallowing, spontaneous eruptions and the crinkling of snack bags, you feel you are a member of the new silent majority in America.

As an out of shape American, I haven't liked what's going on in this country, in a long, long time. I opted not to put up a big fight about it though as the government has taken away all of my supposedly constitutional, inalienable civil rights. I mean free speech, privacy, freedom to worship and protection against unlawful arrests, searches and seizures were great, but, to be completely honest, exercising my rights always made me feel kind of hungry and exhausted anyway.

You consider yourself at the forefront of a new wave of millennial type of American body builders, yet have been completely ostracized by the traditional body building world. You suspect those meatheads are just insanely jealous of your rapidly growing fan base and your wildly popular method of building your body with a daily 10,000 calorie diet of Big Macs, Cheetos, Twinkies and Yoo Hoo's.

When a marriage is on the rocks as your active lifestyles decline, most marriage counselors in America will surprisingly advise their chubby clients to visit All U Can Eat buffets on a regular basis to save the marriage. Oddly enough, the couples who try this usually fall in love all over again when they discover they really do enjoy each other's company again when they're doing activities they both love that are fattening.

Due to the rapid expansion of humongous monstrosities forming in America these days, the plastic surgery market is exploding due to a new procedure for non-religious, double chin foreskin circumcisions.

In a normal marriage, the wife is a clothes hoarder and always has a jam-packed closet full of clothes. That's why an odd feature of a long and happy American marriage is when there are 8 different sizes of pants in her closet but they are all hers.

You're overweight if you have trouble fitting into an airplane bathroom. You're a distinct, "never before in the history of humanity" American level of overweight if you have trouble fitting through the barn door of the bathroom at your favorite All U Can Eat buffet.

There's been such an explosive epidemic of obesity in America, it's only a matter of time before Congress is forced to write a bill to make it a federal hate crime of aggravated assault for smooshing people on planes. If that were to happen, your worst fear is you'd never be able to fly again without incriminating yourself at least 5 times by the time you start squooshing row 3.

You may be an overweight American if you doctored the lyrics of your favorite theme song to: "Yes there were times, I'm sure you knew, I bit off more than I could chew, but through it all, I stood tall and ate it all, and ate it MY WAY".

The indisputable success of America's world-leading, food service economy is a testament to one of our most cherished inalienable rights. Constitutionally, we protect each citizen's right to enjoy the most popular leisure time activity for most Americans in the pursuit of happiness which, of course, is doing things that are fattening. I'm sure the lofty Declaration of Independence sounded really cool at the time, but if our Founding Fathers were alive today, as a group I'm sure they would unanimously agree "Didn't see that one coming."

If this is what it takes, you're in favor of risking another bloody revolutionary war to protect the revised inalienable rights of America's rapidly growing, silently munching majority by establishing the world's first Freedom Fighter's Obesitocracy. You're convinced our Founding Fathers would support your principled, revolutionary call to action of like-minded pudgy patriots to force the government to represent all citizens equally by changing our motto from 'In God We Trust' to 'All U Can Eat'.

Marriage is tough for any couple but it's even harder for most Americans and leaves no wonder why our divorce rate rules the world. The problem is all marriages evolve in some way over time and this can present unforeseen strains on the relationship in the process. In America, the added dilemma for over 90% of couples is they evolve so much, they're forced to try to figure out how they can fit a king-sized marriage into a queen-sized bed.

You make enough to keep your family fed, but, as a tried and true, patriotic American, your constant fear now is about how you'll be able to continue to keep them overfed.

After you've eaten at the July 4th picnic and notice everyone is staring at what you ate in stunned amazement, they're even more shocked when you sit back down to eat again. They couldn't possibly know why, but you've always had a deep and abiding belief that it's the patriotic duty of every true-blooded overweight American to overeat on the birthdate of our nation.

The La-Z-Boy furniture company wants you to be their spokesperson for their fat, dumb and lazy loveseat recliner.

There's only one inalienable right you would defend to the death now as a proud, overweight American. Your greatest hope is your government never dares to establish citizen weight limits without understanding the deadly risk they're running of starting another revolutionary war. There are millions of chubby patriots like you out there who solemnly believe the tree of liberty must be refreshed from time to time with the grease of Big Macs and Whoppers. This modern type of revolutionary is willing to risk death in food fights at McDonalds over the healthy choice menu and is committed to the modern warrior's motto of "Give me meals with 1000% of my daily allowance of hydrogenated, saturated fats or give me death!"

You may be an overweight American if your driver instructor assumes correctly that most of your driver training should be done mastering parallel parking and 3 point turns in and out of McDonald's drive thru's.

Before the 21st century, a wimp in America had always been commonly known as a 98-pound weakling. With the modern wonders of previously inconceivable weight gain for a human being, we owe it to our fast food economy that this same wimp in modern times is now known as a 398-pound weakling.

Most of the world's people consider themselves over-weight when they can't find anything in their closet that fits. Americans finally admit they could stand to lose a few pounds when they can't even squeeze their way into the closet to find out nothing fits anymore.

The sheer size of the enormous butts so many American women are shamelessly putting on full public display in yoga pants these days is perplexing. As a result, it's not at all ridiculous to conclude there's got to be some new vision disorder sweeping over America that's strangely afflicting only women with big butts. What else could explain this phenomenon? After somehow smooshing all that butt into a teeny pair of yoga pants that look like they're about to explode, how is it even possible these women can think "My butt is lookin' gooood"? My guess is it's an optical illusion like one of those side view car mirrors. What else could allow them to go out looking so ridiculous other than a new, nearsighted 'Objects in the mirror appear smaller than their actual, humongous size' vision disorder?

Japan is furious that they're being made to be the laughingstock of the world now that the United States has started its own professional Sumo wrestling league. As if it wasn't insulting enough to their ancient tradition that our combatants are allowed to eat Grubhub deliveries during their matches, we've also committed the ultimate sacrilege with our fighting attire. Our Sumo wrestling stars wisely refused to wear the traditional diaper of the sport, knowing comedians would have such a field day with that the fledgling sport might not be able to survive in America. By wearing enormous, Fruit of the Loom whitey tighties, our greatest stars in the sport have added a more respectable, modern look to the uniform. A surprise, added benefit to this change is they've also revolutionized the ancient belly bumping rules of victory by adding the wildly popular 'Atomic Wedgie' technique to win the match.

My greatest fear in modern America is to show up in a TikTok video with 10 million views of me in a very compromising position. If you think I'm talking about a sex video, that's nothing compared to the shame of becoming infamous for being engaged in a Karma Sutra pose with one of the Legendary Asses of Walmart. It's not well-known, but a lot of the hippopotamic land masses you see grazing in the snack aisle are actually on the payroll of TikTok'ers. Once they identify a sucker like you, all they need to hear are those magic words "Would you mind if I squeeze by?", as they're blocking an entire aisle, and they've got you just where they want you. In that instant, you've just exposed yourself to the real potential of becoming a worldwide internet sensation 10 minutes later on the 'Asses of Walmart'. It's all because the hidden TikTok'er captured you submerged in her butt crack in a doggy style pose just as she leaned over to pick up a 3-pound bag of Doritos on the bottom shelf as you tried to squeeze by.

Everyone in my Overeater's Anonymous group is hyper-sensitive about their weight and doesn't want anyone to know they belong to a group like this. When I tried to tell them it defeats the purpose of trying to be discreet about our group if we insist on meeting at a restaurant, no one paid any attention to my concern. If that wasn't bad enough, we meet on Friday's from 8:00 a.m. to 8:00 p.m. and everyone wears their Golden Corral Hall of Fame Overeaters of America t-shirts. Just to seem polite, some people agreed that they saw my point, but when we voted on changing the location, the bottomless anonymous were unanimous the answer was "Not just 'no' but 'Hell no!'".

When Americans finally upgrade to king-sized beds, they're basically being honest with themselves that none of the 50 diets they have been on have helped, even a little. Furthermore, deep down they know no other diet will ever work unless they get tough on themselves and start eating right and exercising. At this pivotal moment in their lives, they're faced with the stark reality of the Spartan discipline that's an absolute necessity to even have a prayer of achieving any weight loss success. This is the moment, in the new tradition of modern Americans, they conclude "Awwww hell, who am I kiddin' anyway? I ain't doin' all that bullshit. I guess what I really needed all this time is a bigger bed to go with my bigger truck, bigger doorways and bigger 'One size fits all' overalls."

After all the sedentary binging activities most Americans did during the COVID self-quarantine, I guess I was naïve about the inevitable transformation I thought would result in society. Based on the tremors I'd feel as brontosaurus-sized neighbors trudged past my house, I would have sworn there would be an explosion of competitive eating contests, 'Big and Fat' clothes store stock topping the New York stock exchange and American Sumo wrestling gym chains opening all over the country. Other than a massive increase in Grubhub deliveries since then though, there hasn't been a peep out of any tubbo who is willing to lead this revolution. It's truly perplexing and I can only guess as to why the new silent majority has been so silent. Could it be, after all this time has passed since the pandemic ended, that they still can't squeeze out their front door yet?

Despite all the fear tactics skinny doctors like to use to scare fat people to eat less, lose weight and exercise, you can tell most overweight Americans aren't listening to a word they say. In fact, from what I can see, they're actually doubling down on the likelihood of their future circumferential expansion. How else can you explain that when you go to a furniture store in America now looking for a twin-size bed, they still sell them, but their width has been updated to 2 king-size beds?

With all the dumpster-sized Americans you have to negotiate your way around everywhere you go now, it's only a matter of time before Congress enacts some much-needed laws to address 'Felonious Fat Fanny' assaults. To show they're serious, the first action of Congress should be to make it a federal hate crime when an aggravated assault involves pre-meditated ass bumping that causes skinny people to crash into floor displays at Walmart. An insincere "Sorry, I can't see what my butt is bumping into on wide right turns" apology is just not enough justice anymore when your reputation is ruined 15 minutes later as this 'unavoidable accident' reaches one million views on Instagram.

Barbers are retiring at an alarming rate in America these days because of our rapidly growing obesity problem. Throughout their careers, they learned to live with the hassles of cutting extra shoulder hair, along with free eyebrow, nose and ear hair as part of the fixed price for middle-aged guys. Due to the growing epidemic of customers who have titanic butt cheeks where shoulder blades should be though, barbers are quitting in droves to preserve some semblance of their self-respect. Before they would ever advertise that they do free butt crack trimming now, most of them would rather remove matted tud balls at Pet Smart so they closed the shop and became dog groomers.

I would fear for our country's future if we didn't have the most technologically advanced military the world has ever seen. Most of the legendary, feared and admired American fighting men from wars past have been replaced by human land masses who are only willing to fight and die in a buffet line by bumping bellies over the last piece of pumpkin pie. The United States is so fat now, they had to stop teaching 'hand to hand' combat in the trenches and have begun teaching 'hand to mouth' eating contest combat in the mess hall. Thank God we have all these amazing, advanced weapon systems to wipe out any foe that presents a clear and present danger. Otherwise, we'd most likely end up having to resolve all our military conflicts by challenging our greatest enemies to food fights at All U Can Eat battlefields.

You have a rare condition unique to overweight Americans called Burger Kingitis. When you have this rapidly spreading condition, the telltale symptom at the drive thru pick up window is it looks like your air bag inflated in the crotch of your pants. You also develop a temporary hearing disorder that prevents you from hearing what they're saying on the drive thru intercom because your butt cheeks cover your ears now when you're driving. Thankfully, the Burger King drive thru attendants have all been trained to recognize this medical condition and take alternate steps. Before you can begin to panic about not having enough room for your order, they put a 2-foot, flexible straw into your 48-ounce Super-sized chocolate milk shake and place it in your exposed, butt crack cup holder before you drive off.

For the first time in your life, you have a sense of what our Forefathers were willing to fight and die for now that you feel your modern civil rights have been infringed upon. You've never felt like this before and think you must have been inspired from the ghosts of our forefathers past, who preferred death rather than tolerate the tyranny you're under the thumb of now. As much of a shock as it is for you, a sedentary couch potato, you're willing to pledge your life, your fortune and your sacred honor, to establish a new, inalienable freedom in our constitution. As the Patrick Henry of our age, you've vowed not to rest until they give you liberty, to eat all you can eat by abolishing closing times at 24/7 diners, or give you death, from a 30-minute hunger strike.

Japan must live in abject fear our American Walmart heavyweights might unite one day and decide to take over the International Sumo Wrestling Federation. If that ever happened, all of Japan's current worldwide superstars would end up facing the humiliation of competing in the new Sumo Flyweight division that no one but no one watches. Meanwhile, the super-heavyweight division would become dominated by Walmart's finest fatsoes who would revolutionize the ancient arts of Sumo wrestling techniques. While holding a Big Mac in one hand and a super-sized order of fries in the other, they would make a laughingstock of each alleged, legendary Japanese 'warrior'. Those guys wouldn't have a chance. After they're paralyzed momentarily from the stench of a combined McDonald's belch and fart, they'd soon be sailing to Palookaville with the signature American knockout technique of a combination of man boob upper cuts followed by a butt cheek home run into the bleachers.

Have you noticed Japan is rapidly losing their interest in Sumo wrestling when this sport used to be the pride and joy of their reputation on the world stage? Sadly, their best wrestlers have faced the facts and realize it's only a matter of time before American 'Faces of Walmart' star shoppers take an interest in the sport. Once that happens, the weight classes they've maintained for hundreds of years will collapse overnight and all of their best current superheavyweights are going to have to bear the dishonor of moving into a new flyweight division.

Trust me, no business really gives a crap about their supposedly valued customers, other than how they impact profits. Take McDonalds for instance. They're on a health food kick these days, as if they've grown a conscience out of concern for their customers' welfare. Now they're allegedly all caught up in the medical industry's hype about needing to lessen salts, preservatives and fats in their meals because of the damaging effects they 'might' be having on their best customers. That's the respectable way they represent themselves in public now. In their secret meetings though, they haven't suddenly found compassion and become worried sick about the millions of fatsoes they've littered the land with for the past 80 years. They're just terrified they've been so fabulously successful at creating human land masses - the likes of which have never before been seen in humanity - with their secret, addictive additives that sales are plummeting because their all-time best customers can't even fit through the double doors anymore.

You can tell Americans are getting fatter by a drastic change in an old honeymoon tradition that's been time-honored for years. Most new husbands have good intentions to follow the tradition of carrying their new bride across the threshold and into their honeymoon suite, but usually can't even get one of these hefty modern wives to budge when he tries to lift her. That's what prompted the change in the tradition. Nowadays, a newlywed husband huddles his groomsmen outside the door of his hotel room. After he calls the play, they get in stances for a "4th and goal to go" offensive line formation. On the snap, they crash into the new blushing bride's butt and 'tush push' her until she squeezes through the doorway. It's only then the groom can finally be left alone with his new bride to start celebrating the honeymoon by going for a 2-point conversion for the game winning score.

Unlawful aisle imprisonment is a condition unique to Walmart where your civil rights are violated when you are illegally detained without being charged. It usually occurs when you try to run into the store for 5 minutes to buy a pack of gum or something in the candy aisle and forgot to plan an escape route. Due to this unforgivable oversight, you only have yourself to blame that you end up leaving 2 hours later. The untimely delay was caused by the failure of multiple desperate attempts to squeeze by the legendary 'Asses of Walmart' customers who are on both ends of the aisle leisurely grazing in the 'bag your own' chocolates section.

You've always been an eater, not a fighter, but lately you've been filled with such a patriotic fervor, it thrills and frightens you at the same time. After much soul searching, you believe that unless congress acts now the only answer for you and millions of others like you is another revolutionary war in America to create the world's first Obesitocracy. After all, America's largest voting bloc believes the Tree of Liberty needs to be watered at times with the blood from a big, juicy Double Whopper. Unless we memorialize a democratic form of government that establishes overeating rights that are of the fat people, for the fat people and by the fat people, I fear us fat guys are one day going to perish from the earth.

I really don't have anything against fat people, but I do believe it's high time we make new obesity laws for these changing times to protect the public safety. This is why license plates and flashing warning signs should be required to be worn on the back of every 400+ pound customer at Walmart as they enter the store. The sign should say "WARNING!!! if you can't see my elbows, I can't see what my butt is bumping into on wide right turns." I mean why should anyone be allowed to smoosh you into a floor display you had just been innocently checking prices at a moment before and leave your crumpled body lying on a pile of Hormel chili cans? After it happened to me, security guards asked if I got the plate of the truck that must have hit me. All I could tell them was "There wasn't a plate, but it did say 'World's #1 Biggest Butt!!!' on the back of her yoga pants." It turned out that was no help because they told me at any given time in the store at least 50 women are wearing those identical yoga pants.

It's amazing to me that even though there are more humongous people around now than ever before, not only are they not self-conscious about it they seem proud to be 'Made in America'. How else could someone like my chubby brother-in-law brag "Watch this. For my next feat, I'm going to make a butt dial from the phone of that complete stranger across the lobby and call my own phone."

If Jesus lived in modern America and had overweight, overeating Americans for apostles, can you imagine what it would have been like to be at the table with him at the Last Supper? Just think of it: the entire history of Christianity as we know it would be irreversibly altered. As the Last Supper ended and Jesus was about to pass a loaf of bread around and ask his apostles to eat it in memory of him, he would look a little miffed and say "Don't tell me you guys ate all the bread again. Didn't anyone hear me say to save one loaf for the end of the meal because I had something really important to say? Geesh!" After that, he would have had no choice but to change the solemn tradition of the breaking of bread at every mass by saying "Here, take and eat these after-dinner mints - because SOMEONE ate all the bread - and eat them in memory of me."

3

———————————————

BRAZILIAN BUTT LIFT BUTT CHEEK EAR WARMERS

YOUR BUTT IS so big, it takes so long to smell one of your own farts you usually think someone else did it once you finally get a whiff.

When you're sitting on a friend's couch and his wife comes in all frantic because her precious kitty is missing, all you can think is "Here we go again. I hope they find the stupid cat soon before she asks if I wouldn't mind if they check between my butt cheeks again".

Your butt is so big, some farts get lost trying to make their way out your ass and end up as burps instead.

Your butt has gotten so big, after you sit on the couch the back of your head smells like your butt crack.

You can always tell when a guy's butt has gotten so humongous that his farts have trouble finding their way out of his ass so they're forced to look for alternate exit routes. The telltale sign for this is when you see one of these guys absent-mindedly doing armpit farts to avoid getting bloated.

You realize your butt must have grown a lot more than you feared when your Proctologist put an overtime charge on your annual exam.

When you were young and carefree, you always thought it would be sexy to grow your hair down to your butt one day. As you developed a liking for junk food though, you realized as you got older that it was much easier to grow your butt up to your hair.

The only time you're absolutely sure you've been butting into someone else's business is when you hear muffled screams for help beneath one of your butt cheeks.

Your wife knows you always loved staring at her ass when you were young. Now that you're older and your vision isn't so good anymore, she told you that she self-lessly grew her butt much bigger - just for you - so you wouldn't have trouble trying to see it.

Your police department has taken out warrants to search your butt crack for missing pets.

Your butt is so big, farts give up trying to find their way out of your ass and become sneezing farts instead.

You've advanced from just being considered fat to humongous status when you look like you have another butt crack anywhere else on your body other than where an actual butt crack should be.

You had to stop doing the popular 'Buns of Steel' workout program when your butt began resembling a life-sized battleship.

When the nicest thing you can say about her is that she has a huge heart, you can bet it's nowhere as big as her huge ass.

When you ask your husband "Do you think these pants make my butt look big?", he says "Sorry for pointing out a technicality, but don't you mean bigger?" When you don't answer, but start throwing plates at him, he knows that really is what she meant.

You don't complain to your husband about him leaving the toilet seat up all the time anymore because you've grown your butt big enough now to be able to go to the bathroom without it.

You've developed a hearing problem, but it only happens when you're driving. You have a strong suspicion you know how it's happening because you can't ever remember a time before when your butt cheeks covered your ears.

Your wife has become so concerned about the troubling expansion of her butt, you had to buy her an 'objects appear smaller than actual size' vanity mirror for the bedroom.

Guys used to stand still and stare at your captivating ass when you were young and in shape. Now that you're no longer young or in shape, you catch them leaning awkwardly sideways trying to see around it.

Guys still stare at your butt when you wear jeans like they used to when you were in great shape in your 20's. Nowadays though, it's more likely that they're only doing it because they're completely baffled about the 3 butt cracks they're seeing and think they must be some kind of an optical illusion.

You're not stupid, but when you sit anywhere nowadays you really have to be careful to avoid being laughed at for having your head up your ass whenever you get it stuck in your butt crack.

You know your ass has gotten way too big whenever you fart while you're sitting down and you can feel it ricochet off the back of your head on its way out.

Your butt cheeks rest so high up on your back now when you sit, people always know when you're the one who farted when they see your ears flutter.

Your ponytail is only 6 inches long but you're going to get it cut off at your hair dresser's because you're sick and tired of it getting stuck in your butt crack when you're in the tub.

When guys stare at your butt at a bar now, it's only because they're having weird thoughts like "If I'm very quiet and careful, I wonder if I could use her butt crack as a beer koozie without her even noticing?"

As of this writing, there have been no known spontaneous explosions of yoga pants incidents yet while they were stretched to the max over a Walmart-sized butt, but why take a chance trying to be stylish? It would be wise to switch to a Snuggie if you're ever asked at a bar "Excuse me ma'am, there's no room to put our beers down anywhere while we play pool. If you're going to be standing there for a while, would you mind if we left them on your butt cheek shelf?"

Every time you sneeze now your butt dials someone you didn't want to talk to and then it never fails that one of your man boobs always seems to hang up before you can apologize you have the wrong number.

Instead of holding a hand to your ear like normal people do to indicate they can't hear someone, you take both hands and pull your butt cheeks away from your ears and then say "Pardon me, can you repeat that last part?".

Butt dials are an embarrassing sign you're overweight. A muffled ringing sound from your butt when you can't find your phone is a uniquely American overweight condition.

When you're sitting now and have an itchy neck, you have to carefully reach back to locate it so you don't end up accidentally scratching one of your ass cheeks instead.

Your husband is such a show off, you're forced to tell him at social gatherings "I know I told you it was okay to do it when we're alone on the couch at home while we're watching a movie, but not at a party. You're embarrassing me when you show off by letting everyone know my butt crack makes a great beer koozie. Right now, besides yours, I have no idea who the other 5 beers in there even belong to."

The most fascinating thing about you is when you fart in vinyl chairs the rushing wind makes your ear lobes flutter as it passes.

You've noticed lately that you're having trouble hearing when you order at the drive thru, but then realize it improves when you pull one of your butt cheeks away from an ear and say "Sorry, did you ask if I wanted to super-size my order? I didn't hear you the first time."

When you were young and sexy, you used to love the reaction you got out of your husband when you asked him teasingly "How does my butt look in these new pants?" You never ask his opinion anymore though since 'the date that will last in infamy' when he said "Woman, are you trying to set me up to look like a damn fool or something? How in tarnation am I supposed to give you an opinion on how your butt looks in the pants when, from what I'm seeing, you've only been able to stuff about half of it in them so far?"

Your butt has grown so much, you've stopped asking your husband "Do you think these pants make my butt look big?" and now ask "Do you think our teeny house is making my butt look bigger?"

It was so ironic that you became depressed when you realized you could no longer reach down far enough to tie your shoes anymore, yet, no sooner than you started to sulk about it, you cheered yourself up when you noticed you're able to kiss your own ass now.

There's no reason for anyone to sneak a peek at your butt anymore when it's usually causing a partial eclipse now.

Whenever your husband accuses you of blowing things way out of proportion during an argument, you think the subject has shifted to the size of your butt.

Your ass hangs so low now, it's so much less embarrassing when you accidentally fart in public because people just think it must be your feet that stink.

My wife is ecstatic about how great her butt looks in our new 'objects in the mirror appear smaller than actual size' bedroom mirror. Of course this has made me extremely self-conscious about ever making the humiliating mistake again of dropping my shower towel in front of it.

Your barber refuses to shave the back of your neck anymore when you're getting a haircut because he says it's not his job to have his 2 assistant barbers pull your ass cheeks out of the way for him to be able to trim it.

Your butt cheeks go so high up your back now when you sit, your hairdresser has to ask you to pull your pony tail out of your butt crack before she'll trim it.

You have so much ass in front now, the locker room bully at your gym has no idea where to grab your underwear's waistband to give you a wedgie.

You've inadvertently helped co-workers understand the astronomical phenomenon of Black Holes better. It's like they're stargazing as they watch the ankle length skirt you wore to work transform into a miniskirt as more and more of the skirt's dark matter disappears into the deep space of your mysterious butt cheek vortex all day long.

Friends fear talking behind your back now because they've heard the terrifying rumors about the buffet gases that can spontaneously combust without warning back there when you flick your lighter because you think someone is gossiping about you.

The greatest compliment Lululemon design engineers could ever receive is hearing the amazement women express to one another at Walmart about the seemingly infinite elasticity of their yoga pants when they ask "How in the world did you ever fit all that butt into those teeny pants?" and get the reply "Look who's talking."

The person sitting behind you at the movie theater asks if you would kindly remove your hat so he's able to see the movie between your butt cheeks.

The only reason people would ever stare at you with wonder is when they're wondering how you manage to wipe your own butt.

When you wake up with a stiff neck, nothing provides fast relief like leaning your head back and resting it for a while in the radiant heat from your butt crack neck brace.

When co-workers talk about the possibility of carpooling with you, they don't exactly spell out what they mean when they say "We all think you're a wonderful co-worker and we'd love to do that… except there's one 'big butt' involved that would likely make it impractical."

Your butt is so big it doesn't even look any smaller anymore in 'objects appear smaller than their actual size' mirrors.

When you see the size of the butts that American women are trying to stuff into yoga pants that are 3 sizes too small, you can't help but assume there must be a new, rapidly spreading 'objects appear smaller than actual size' vision problem that's strangely afflicted only American women in front of their bedroom mirrors.

You know you're not so insecure about your weight anymore because you used to have a terrified look, but now just get a self-loathing look whenever you see yourself naked in a mirror.

Surprisingly, you have very distinct tastes for a fat guy. At your favorite type of restaurant, all the patrons have butt cheeks where shoulder blades should be.

You know you're fat when you start making butt dials all the time. You're at a whole new level of fat when your butt is starting to make butt dials on other people's phones.

The indisputably ironic evidence can be seen everywhere now that one of the most common characteristics of 90% of women who currently wear yoga pants in public is they couldn't fit into a yoga class while they are wearing them.

I don't think my wife read all the product warnings before she began the Brazilian butt lift workout last winter. The change in her was amazing, but she must have missed some small print somewhere that said the workout is only designed to lift the butt, not make it any smaller. That's why in the Spring all her friends said she looked great in her new Capris, even though she was still wearing all her old 'fat' pants. She's actually on the Brazilian butt lift reversal program now, but it doesn't have anything to do with her pants. She also didn't realize that when the butt lift program is successful for a woman with an enormous butt, they can get temporary hearing problems from a condition called Butt Cheek Ear Muff Central Auditory Processing Disorder.

Your husband used to wait on you hand and foot, but completely stopped once you grew an enormous butt. When you became worried about this and asked if he didn't love you anymore, he told you "You've got it all wrong honey, I still love you more than anything else in the world. You're still my one and only true love and always will be. I just stopped kissing your ass all the time though because that's what I thought might have been the reason it had grown so much." Somehow this wasn't the comforting response you'd hoped for.

There is a magical period during every holiday season when most women experience a delightful suspension of reality due to the extra heaping helpings of peace on earth and goodwill towards men. This temporary insanity somehow allows them to believe they can scarf down an extra 3000 cookie and dessert calories a day for 6 weeks without consequence to their butt size. I admit I can't explain it, but I've observed somehow their wishes get magically granted by some unknown gods of holiday festivities. The holiday season ends on January 1 though and payback is a bitch. At some point late in the afternoon on that day, you will hear a loud BOIINNNGGG!!! noise coming from the bedroom followed by the eery sound hip hugger jeans make when they're being shredded from a sudden explosion. Even though this

BOIINNNGGG is much louder and more frightening than the first time you heard it after taking the CVS generic brand of Viagra, do not – I repeat – do not go in there if you know what's good for you.

4

WHAT TO EXPECT WHEN IT ONLY LOOKS LIKE HE'S EXPECTING

FOR SOMEONE IN your terrible shape, you were reminded once again of the painful consequences you experience when you don't properly plan to avoid getting yourself into dire predicaments that most people never even have to think about. This dawned on you one day as you were constipated and sitting in a port o' potty at your son's Little League baseball game. You suddenly realized, if you barely fit into it in the first place, how in the world did you convince yourself you'd be able to squeeze back out after you had a pizza delivered?

What most women in their 40's fail to grasp when they say they want to get their old figure back is that they actually never lost it; it's been with them all along. What they fail to realize is it's just trapped beneath 6 sedimentary dessert layers of other figures they've added on top of the original one.

When you turn 40 and you're looking to have a "I'm looking at the man in the mirror" honest moment with yourself, to avoid confusion, you're probably better off only looking from the neck up if your man boobs have already progressed past the training bra stage.

I wouldn't call it a mid-life crisis, but it was clearly an indication I'd already reached the peak of my masculinity in life and am now on a steep decline when my wife asked me if I wanted to go try on bras at the mall for my 40th birthday present.

In my late 30's I stopped going to the beach when I became very insecure and ashamed when my man chest had reached a deeply concerning training bra level of flabbiness. I'm over that childish fear now that I'm in my 40's and have developed fully matured, double D cup man boobs. Instead of the insecurity that used to haunt me, I'm much more worried now that I might be getting a little too conceited about my new look. I finally know what it's like for a woman now to try not to let it go to your head when I catch women gawking at my cleavage all the time whenever I'm wearing a V-neck shirt over my new push-up bro.

I would never tell anyone about the male push-up bra I secretly wear that I bought at Victor's Secrets. Although I had some deep misgivings about wearing one, I ended up buying it because I was so desperate to keep my D cup man boobs from making me a laughingstock in public in any shirt I wore. The difference in my self-confidence has been truly life changing. Now that I have an attractive, shapely cleavage in V-neck t-shirts, it's like I'm the most popular jock in high school again. I can tell the 'pumping iron' meatheads who used to ridicule me at any chance are all impressed now when they make the ultimate buff guy comment "Nice pecs, dude. How much do you bench?"

The effect the laws of physics have on the body over 50 years are cruel and unequal to women. As a guy, I'm not happy the hair that used to be on my head made a migration south and found retirement homes on my eyebrows, shoulders, ears, nose and back. I would gladly opt for my dilemma any day though compared to a woman in her 50's having to explain how her 36-24-36 figure became a 24-36-48 when unrelenting gravitational forces caused her boobs to morph into her butt.

When you walk past a new customer in the lobby as you're leaving the Weight Watchers you've been a member of for the last 20 years, the receptionist always whispers to him "You're the 2nd new customer today who's here for your 'Before' picture. You just passed the first guy as you were coming in."

40 is that wonderful age of excitement for a guy when he celebrates this birthday and then wonders with breathless anticipation which will come first: male pattern baldness or male pattern boobiness.

You used to complain to your husband all the time that you hate your figure since you became a mother, just to try to coax some compassionate support out of him. He's still supportive, but now he tells you "What's the big deal about it anyway honey? Me? I personally love ovals. They're probably my favorite figures. If you don't believe me, let me remind you that footballs are oval-shaped."

When you tell people you're out of shape, they wonder if you must mean that your current oval-shape used to be more pear-shaped.

You're so out of shape, you don't even have to roll over in your sleep anymore. Your rolls roll you over on their own now.

You were always an A student in math when you were in school, but admitted to your wife that you were completely baffled about the variables in her eating equation that could have caused her geometrical figure to unexpectedly change from an hourglass to an oval almost overnight.

Your wife is absolutely freaking out and is insisting on a boob job now that she knows there's no contest your man boobs are bigger than hers.

I've noticed that the disturbing changes in my wife's figure over the years have had a negative effect on me too. I know I used to be a liar but, to be able to live in peaceful harmony, I'm a bigger one now than I ever was before.

You were absolutely thrilled when you realized that co-workers noticed you had been in the best shape of your life when they all started telling you "I'm getting concerned about you. You look like you're really starting to let yourself go."

Your old hourglass figure looks more like one that would measure the 24 hours in a day now.

You've asked your preacher for the church's position on double-chin circumcisions.

You're trying to get back into a little better shape because you know the first thing God is going to say when he meets you on Judgment Day is "Before you hear your judgment, drop and give me 20, fatso".

10 years later, you still eat a ½ gallon of chocolate chip, double fudge swirl ice cream every night with a jar of pickles before going to bed. It's all because you have never been able to overcome the trauma of the sympathy pains you heroically endured for your wife when she was pregnant.

You're so out of shape, when you accidentally bump into old friends now, you don't get a chance to say hello because you weren't even aware your butt bumped them into a different time zone.

When you swim, the lifeguards at the pool are required to post a tsunami warning flag.

You are so better in touch than ever before with a woman's unique vulnerabilities now that you know what it's like to feel violated when women sneak lewd peeks at your man boob cleavage.

You can't tell which is a more alarming indicator of your rapid weight gain: how fast your breast cleavage is sinking or how high your ass cleavage has already risen.

It's embarrassing to have to admit it to yourself, but you have to start shopping confidentially at Victor's Secrets now for man boob bras because of Walmart's discriminatory practice of not offering a lingerie section for the overweight, middle-aged male.

When you met up with a dear old friend you hadn't seen in ages and he told you "Wow, you look like you're really starting to let yourself go.", you were deeply embarrassed. All you could say was "Boy do I feel terrible. I guess it's been a lot longer than I thought since we last saw each other because I started letting myself go years ago."

You've unnecessarily corrected a co-worker to try to preserve some trace of your self-respect when you were told that you must have accidentally butt dialed her by telling her "I hate to correct you, but it was actually a sagging man boob that made that accidental call."

Your male-pattern boobiness has passed the training bra stage.

There's no question it would be a multi-million dollar New York Times best seller, but no male dietician would ever have the balls to write the diet book that so many American women could obviously use titled "What to Expect When It Just Looks Like You're Expecting".

People never buy your explanation that all of your weight gain was the result of sympathy pain binge eating during your wife's pregnancies, unless their calculation was right and they believe you actually do have at least 30 kids.

Your wife thought it was so precious how you grew a sympathy pain belly like hers when she was pregnant. 15 years later, she's not buying the sympathy pain act about why you grew the saggy man boobs out of sympathy because she always looks like she might be pregnant now.

You'll dare to go where no man has gone before, but it's only because you don't fit into most public bathroom stalls when you've really got to pee.

I was a really fat kid when I was young. Like most moms, I wasn't allowed by mine to go back in the water at the pool until I waited for one hour. For me though, I had to wait until I had digested enough so I could fit back in.

You're okay with swimming right after eating, but always wait one hour after eating before you'll drive. On average, that's usually the amount of digestion time it takes for your belly to recede enough so you can steer again.

As you were saying your goodbyes, you always used to tell interesting people you'd just met "I sure hope I bump into you again sometime soon". Now that you've gained a ton of weight, you had to stop saying that. Your lawyer advised you your friendly goodbye could actually end up as a goldmine for a billboard personal injury lawyer who could use it as a confession for a premeditated, felony for assault and butt battery.

Have you ever noticed how guys with enormous butts tend to linger around for a while at a restaurant with a lost expression after their plates are gone and the bill has been paid? Even if it's awkward when the waiters are wondering why they haven't left yet, they've learned from experience it's advisable to stay for a while to digest if they know what's good for them. Each of them knows they want to avoid getting flooded with texts from friends - again - letting him know there's already one million views on Instagram of him waddling out of the restaurant with a chair stuck to his butt.

You never try to get a laugh by insulting anyone in public anymore because, just when you think you've just delivered the perfect zinger, some wiseguy always ends up telling you "Heh buddy, why don't you try picking on someone your own size?" and everyone starts belly laughing about that instead.

At highway rest stops, you turn and ask the surprised guy standing next to you "Don't take this the wrong way, pal. I'm definitely not one of those pervs you hear about in these places trying to proposition you or anything like that. I'm just hoping you could give me a little assistance. To avoid the embarrassment of me having to apologize for pissing on your shoes, would you mind taking a quick peek and tell me if I'm even close to aiming at the urinal?"

When you go for a quick dip in the ocean, everyone who had come to the beach at that time because they thought the tide was supposed to be going out was wondering why it was coming in again.

Now that you've got them, your doctor advised that it couldn't hurt for you to start doing a monthly man boob breast exam until your Ozempic prescription starts working.

Zoo hippos look at you curiously wondering how in the world you managed to get yourself on the other side of the fence.

You're not religious, but you're pretty confident, if they had a high enough ladder, you could part the Red Sea as well as Moses did with one of your atomic cannonballs.

Your wife is ashamed to be seen with you in public but it's only because you lost weight on the diet she gained 10 pounds on and now she thinks that would just make her look even bigger.

They were going to arrest you at the beach for public nudity until you lifted your belly and showed them the bathing suit you were wearing.

Because you just never seem to learn your lesson about the risk of eating your lunch in confined spaces, at least once a month you're forced to depend on the kindness of strangers to help remove the porta potty that's stuck to your butt.

If you had your choice, you do prefer swimming in lakes, but feel limited to only swim in the ocean now because the beach front property doesn't flood as bad as it does at the lake.

The New Jersey lifeguards whistled for you to stop splashing because they were getting tsunami warnings from the lifeguards in West Africa.

You told friends that you went to the beach for the day, but strangers who saw you there assumed you were beached for the day.

When you joined a Weight Watchers activity group that was going bungee jumping for the first time, you thought it would be wise to make absolutely sure you were jumping from a safe height. You decided the best way would be to check with the group activity director so you asked her "Before I jump, I know it's confidential but would you happen to know the approximate weights of the 3 group members who jumped before me… you know, the ones whose feet are sticking out of the mud in the creek bed below?"

As an avid sports enthusiast, you're aware there's an unwritten rule of safety in bungee jumping for over-weight people. Whenever you're at a new place and you're getting ready to jump, yet aren't completely sure if the jumping off point is high enough, always remember to follow safety precautions and let the fat, drunken frat guy go first.

As they watch YouTube videos of what happens when you go for a swim in the ocean, religious scholars are beginning to wonder if maybe Moses didn't part the Red Sea after all if there were humongous guys like you around back then. After 3500 years of unquestioned, Exodus doctrine, they believe it's likely the Jewish slaves might have been able to escape from Pharoah's armies across the Red Sea after just one atomic cannonball from a fatso like you who had beefed up on the high-cholesterol Doritos manna.

The cop who was going to cite you for failing to wear a seat belt agreed it was useless for you to wear it when you showed him you had to loop it behind the steering wheel first to get it attached.

Buying the book "What to Expect While She's Expecting" for your wife is thoughtful when she's pregnant. Asking the question "What do you expect when it looks like you're expecting?" when she's not expecting is not.

You scoff at concerned friends who act like they know you when they say "We wanted to get together because we're getting very worried about you. It just seems like you're really starting to let yourself go." When you're confronted like this from the people you thought were your closest friends and they're nervously waiting for a response, all you can come up with is "I appreciate your concern and am deeply sorry I've worried all of you. I have to admit though that if you really knew me as well as you think you do, you would know I made a conscientious decision to start letting myself go years ago."

When it finally dawned on me why everything with our finances was such a mess, I felt a mental thud as I realized "Stupid, stupid stupid…You can't put your wife in charge of the family finances. No matter how hard they try, wives just aren't very good with figures." That's why, if your family budget is anything like the diet plans my wife made to prevent the bankruptcy of her figure, it's probably been through a myriad of gimmicky, hopeless quick fix, diet-type plans, that only make matters worse. Once she's completely disgusted with the depressing figures, like a diet's ending, she'll go on one long, reckless 'binge spending' revenge spree to make it perfectly clear that her days of balancing the family budget figures are over.

For a husband in a long marriage, it's never a big deal for you when your wife announces she's going on a diet and says she's determined to get her old figure back. When you have been married for more than 30 years, the reason you're not excited is you've already experienced at least 6 distinctly different figures on your wife during your time together. When you were young and naïve and heard this for the first time, you were horny as hell that she could only mean she was going to work hard to get her old smokin' hot, Olympian swimmer figure back. Nowadays though, unless by some miracle she actually meant that one, it's hard to get too worked up about this announcement since this time she's most likely just trying to get her oval figure back from her 40's. What's even worse is she doesn't have any of the self-image concerns she had when she was younger, so she usually claims victory and quits now once she's improved to a new beach ball figure that she's never tried before.

I know I've never walked along a high wire while I was blindfolded and juggling flaming hatchets, but I'm certain I know something that's even more dangerous. This, of course, is giving an honest, unrehearsed response to a wife's commentary on her weight or figure. That's why, when a wife of 30 years excitedly announces "I have wonderful news! I'm going on that diet I'm always telling you about to finally get my old figure back. What do you think about that, lover boy?". Of course, the danger to this question is she's had at least 6 different figures since you've known her. Consequently, if you were to respond, however kindly and truthfully you could represent yourself, with the obvious question "Which one, honey?" you don't know how it would end, yet know for sure it wouldn't end well. That's why the only healthy choice is to ignore the question and, as stupid as it sounds, quickly change the subject by saying "That's nice honey... say, have you seen my black blindfold anywhere? I was just about to go out in the back yard and practice that new hobby I think I told you about juggling flaming hatchets."

You hate going to the beach now because it never fails that, just as soon as you start to doze off, a clueless group from Greenpeace rolls you onto a tarp and starts pouring buckets of water on you as they're dragging you to the water to save you. About this time you have a surreal moment as if time were standing still: you're helplessly being dragged to the ocean without a flotation device because your first thought was to grab your 3 pound bag of Cheetos and 2 liter bottle of Mountain Dew, the rescue team is blinded by the coming glory of releasing you back to the ocean and is deaf to your pleas, a large crowd of TikTok'ers have their phones out videotaping the hilarious predicament you're in, when all of a sudden you have a blindingly clear déjà vu moment and all you can think is "Stupid, stupid, stupid. This is the exact same bullshit I had to deal with last year when I came to the beach when I vowed I would never, ever go to the beach again."

You used to love going to the beach, but, now that you've gained a ton of weight, you worry the lifeguards will unfairly discriminate against you again after what happened the last time. Normally, they would just blow their whistle and give you a warning when you were playing too rough in the water. The last time you went, you heard the whistle and saw the lifeguard pointing at you, so you figured you'd be asked to leave the water. This time though, a Frog team of Navy SEALS appeared out of nowhere and rigged you into a net and had a sky crane helicopter drop you on the beach. After they were done interrogating you, thankfully they only gave you a citation for making the terroristic threat of inciting a man-made tsunami. Now you keep a low profile at the beach and will only go ankle wading because you're so worried you'd have to pay a big fine if you were ever dumb enough to do a cannonball off the pier again.

5

PORTA POTTY PIZZA DELIVERIES

YOUR WIFE CAN always tell when you've been out carousing till 2:00 in the morning looking for open drive thru's when she sees the imprint of the steering wheel around your belly button when you try to slip back into bed without being noticed.

Your Smart car bumper sticker says "This vehicle takes slow right turns out of McDonald's parking lots while the steering wheel is pressed against the safe and courteous driver's belly".

You vowed you would never order a pizza from Domino's again after what they told you the last time you called. They rudely informed you, one of the top 10 customers in the United States "Listen pal, we understand your situation, but it's not our problem that you missed lunch because you're constipated. Rules are rules and we're not allowed to make a delivery if the location doesn't have an address. Besides that, we'd look like idiots going around knocking on doors at your son's little league baseball field trying to find the porta potty that you're sitting in."

You're always baffled why there's never anyone standing in line behind you at fast food restaurants. It's because they always leave when they hear what you ordered, figuring correctly that there probably won't be anything left to order once they give you yours.

When you call for a Grubhub delivery, you're always frightening the poor delivery guy half to death by greeting him like he just delivered food from a helicopter at your mountain top crash site after you'd been stranded for 10 days. When he sees you, he says "Take it easy pal. Didn't I just deliver your lunch about 3 hours ago?"

When you order food for home delivery, one of your greatest fears is that one day you'll be excitedly opening the front door after the doorbell rings and you'll see the Grim Reaper standing in front of the delivery guy holding the stack of pizzas you ordered.

You don't eat at McDonalds anymore, but that's only because you can't fit in the store or the drive thru now.

Your best memories all involve food order errors that came out in your favor. That's why your friends always groan whenever you repeat one of your favorite stories that everyone's heard 10 times before. "… Stop me if you've heard this one before but, as I was driving away, I realized the drive thru cashier had given me someone else's order and I ended up with 6 Double Whoppers and 3 orders of supersized fries! Doesn't that just give you a warm and fuzzy feeling all over?" All your closest friends agree and tell you "You're right. It's truly one of the most wonderful, fairy tale love stories I've ever heard for a fat guy like you."

You were the leader of an all-out charge of devout, blood-thirsty crusaders one time, but it was only because you were the first fat guy in line when they opened the door at Krispy Kreme after the red, hot light donut warning came on.

Your wife always knows when you're having constipation problems when you don't show up on time for dinner and then she sees a Domino's pizza delivery guy knocking on your bathroom door.

It doesn't matter what you say to try to comfort a neighbor who invited you to dinner when she asks nervously "Are you sure you've had enough to eat? It wouldn't take much time for me to make some more…I wouldn't want you to leave hungry.", if your pizza delivery order showed up just as she was about to serve dessert.

You think the best time to meet a future wife who shares the same interests as you is when they're having a $1 menu promotion at McDonalds.

You've had a Grubhub order delivered to a men's room stall at a New Jersey turnpike rest stop when you were constipated.

You're the only one who's ever had a restraining order for stalking an ice cream man.

When co-workers lost your address and couldn't reach you, they wisely waited until they saw a Grubhub delivery driver come into the neighborhood and then followed him to your front door. After they told you a BS story about how they actually found the place, you were dumbfounded and said "How in the world does everyone find where I live when I've never given my address out to anyone else at work?"

You've put a finger over your mouth before and whispered angrily "Shhhhh!!!" as you told the pizza delivery driver "Shut your mouth and have a little respect. If you'd even bothered to take a quick look around, who else besides me would have ordered a pizza delivery during an unusually long funeral mass?"

You have Gold club VIP parking at McDonalds that's better than the handicap spots.

Whenever you walk into a Dunkin Donuts, there's always a hushed moment of silence in the room as the regular customers wait to hear what you order.

Your mysterious, seemingly incurable anxiety attacks suddenly stopped immediately a few years back right after your local Wendy's made an announcement that they would be open all night.

When your wife calls as you're leaving work and asks you to pick up the take-out food order, you usually call her at some point on the way home and confess that the smell was too overpowering for your willpower and you ate the entire order. She realizes it's all her fault and could just kick herself, so she places another take out order, but this time it's for home delivery. This allows you to make your normal entrance after work as if nothing had happened and say "Mmmmmmmm…Something smells wonderful. What's for dinner?!?"

When you're in the mood for Chinese food, you give your other loyal fast food suppliers a courtesy call and say "Yeh, it's me, Harvey. Listen, I wanted to give you a heads up that I'm going with Chinese food tonight and there's no way you're going to be able to talk me out of it, so you can let the buffet staff go home early if you want. It's your call."

It seems like you get a lot of telemarketer calls at dinnertime but it's just all your other fast-food joints you didn't select for tonight's take-out order confirming they won't need to keep the staff for an overtime shift.

The only thing that has changed about your lunch in the last 10 years was when they came out with the slogan "Super-sized".

Whenever you're traveling and your wife notices you're starting to get an anxious look like you might be lost, she turns on the GPS and says "Stay calm honey, there's a Krispy Kreme in the next town about 5 miles ahead."

At the KFC suggestion box you wrote "For the love of God, can you move out of the Dark Ages for modern, overweight Americans and change your extra-large order from a bucket to a barrel?".

You hate how you get such a sense of desperation whenever you've felt a hunger pang coming on and you're flat broke. At a time like this, you hate to admit you're no different than any other addict and know you're capable of doing anything to quench your insatiable hunger. It's gotten so bad, you've even worn a ski mask to a neighborhood ice cream truck. When all the kids ran away screaming, you pointed the squirt gun beneath your Snuggie at the ice cream man and said "Give me all your ice cream sandwiches and no one gets hurt."

One of the pathetic aspects of being an overweight family is when we have family funerals. When great grandma passed away recently, it was mostly a beautiful tribute to her life at the funeral service. Unfortunately, the mass went a little too long to expect all of the big eaters to curb their appetites for any length of time. Eventually the solemnity of the service was disrupted during a eulogy that dragged on and on when a pizza delivery guy showed up at the church and started walking up and down the aisles whispering "C'mon guys, I'm just trying to do my job here. Which one of you fatsoes ordered the extra-large meat lovers?"

Neighbors tell you they're sick of the same stupid song you're always playing on your outdoor speakers, but it's actually just the ice cream man making his daily home deliveries at your house.

The pizza delivery guy is allowed to drive the company's armored car with armed security when he delivers to other houses in your neighborhood.

You're so used to ordering fast food at drive thru windows, when you went to pick up your order at the CVS window you said "Can I get supersized #1, #2 and #3 meal combos and an extra-large Vanilla shake with that Ozempic prescription?"

You know your diet is over when you just rear ended someone again - and again -and again – and again

- while you were impatiently waiting in a traffic jam to pick up your order at the Burger King drive thru.

In the superlatives section of your high school class year-book, you were voted "Most Likely to have a road rage, head on collision at a drive thru after they forgot your order of fries".

You order #1, #2, #3 and #4 supersized meals at the Burger King drive thru but only ask for one straw.

You've never had an issue with anxiety attacks, but lately an uncontrollable fear consumes you every time you're in a fast food drive thru line. The ordeal worse than death that you're too scared to even think about is "What would you do if, God forbid, the car in front of you broke down or ran out of gas before you picked up your order?"

Because of the ridiculous amount of time you spend there, you have accepted the truth about your cruel fate that you have an astronomically high probability of dying while waiting to pick up your food in a drive thru lane. That's why, instead of the increasing joy you used to feel as you got closer to the pick-up window, you're always filled with dread now and earnestly pray "Please God, if this is the end for me, have mercy and at least let me eat the French fries!".

Like most angry Americans, you can't help getting more and more road rage these days on the highways. Yours occurs mostly in drive thru lanes though. That's because, when you're driving, you're always too distracted while you're eating to pay any attention to what's going on with the cell phone distracted drivers in the traffic all around you.

You love Chick-fil-A, but hate that their drive thru lines are always so notoriously long. You've learned the only way you can keep your patience while you wait to pick up your order is to have Grubhub deliver an order of Chick-fil-A to you in line so you have something to munch on while you wait.

Your idea of a spine-tingling NASCAR race is driving 250 laps around a Burger King on a Saturday and pitting 10 times at the drive thru pick up window. Nothing gets your cholesterol level pumping faster than seeing the red caution flag being waved out of the pick-up window. This is an indicator of a crash with only 10 laps to go. You know tow trucks will be arriving soon to remove the wreckage, so you gun your engine in a death-defying, record setting lap around the store to get back to the intercom in time to order before the 'temporarily closed' caution flag is raised.

You panicked a little back when you realized you couldn't fit through the McDonald's entrance anymore. You're even more concerned about what you'll survive on now that they've announced, for customer safety reasons, they will no longer allow walk ups in the drive thru lane.

You can always tell when you get that sad, desperate, 'all is lost' look on your face when you've been parked on the side of the highway for more than an hour and your car won't start. Usually some kind stranger will eventually pull over and, after noticing your desolate look, tell you "Heh pal, it's none of my business, but you don't look so good. You look so hungry, you must have been stranded here for days! C'mon, get in. We need to get you to the nearest drive thru CPR before it's too late!!!".

When your car broke down for 3 days recently, all over town the fast food drive thru's had your picture posted at the outdoor menu sign with a candle beneath it.

You've gotten so fat, you tell people you're ashamed to be seen in public now…except, of course, at drive thru's where you're not only treated with respect, but also presumed to be one of their best 400+ pound gold card customers.

To you, an enjoyable dinner and entertainment night out on the town on a rainy day is picking up your 6 bags at the drive thru and then driving around like a vigilante trying to soak joggers next to puddles as you're scarfing down your chow.

Your facial expression is no different than those of starving survivors from a desolate, mountain range plane crash, who incidentally were just rescued from a frigid peak after 3 weeks, whenever you're more than 8th in line at the Burger King drive thru.

Normally you hate to diet but you feel like you've been left with no choice until you lose enough weight to be able to fit back in your car again. Once that happens, you'll be able to stop having food delivered all the time and start going to drive thru's again. That's why you sarcastically call your despised weight loss plan your 'Grubhub diet'. Not only are their deliveries outrageously expensive, you have to tip so much it made you cut 2000 calories off of your usual 10,000 a day because you can't afford to super-size all your orders like you always do at the drive thru.

You're the only customer Burger King has ever issued an unlimited credit gold card to.

Even though you love home-cooked meals every once in a while, it's hard for you to have a peaceful dinner at home because the phone rings constantly whenever you do. As you sit down to eat, all of the local fast-food places start calling and leaving concerned messages like "Harvey – buddy - just calling to let you know me and the entire staff were worried and held a prayer vigil for you when we didn't hear from you today. As you know, you're our most loyal customer and we just wanted to check to see if you need anything and let you know we'll make a courtesy call to 911 if you haven't ordered anything by 5:00 p.m. tomorrow."

There's a McDonald's French fry grease ring in your pool.

You told your regular take-out delivery driver's manager you'd be taking your business elsewhere next time if they refused to protect your privacy by being discreet about the specific delivery instructions. Even though you agreed it was an unusual request, everything was going according to plan at first. After he knocked on the door though, and you whispered "Yeh, it's me" and slipped a $20 bill under the door, the delivery driver couldn't contain himself. He loudly announced to all the soccer moms at the park "Dang! Of all the weird places I've made deliveries to, I have never delivered a pizza to a freakin' porta potty before! Can you believe the tubbo who ordered it told me he knows it's weird but he's constipated and didn't want to be late for dinner?"

You were desperate enough to call Greenpeace for help one time when you were technically beached at McDonald's. After they ganged up to give you the heave-ho out the door, you got very emotional thanking them for saving your life when you were certain all hope was lost and then asked for their business cards. They all looked baffled by your request so you explained "I got stranded, with no hope of survival till you got here, because I was shamefully duped into overeating by McDonald's for promoting a $5 dollar Meal Deal with unlimited $1 dollar extra meals all day after that. What else was a guy like me supposed to do with a golden opportunity like this?". They thanked you for the explanation, but still seemed confused about why you would need their business cards so you told them "Don't you see? The promotion isn't over for a few days so I figured I'll probably need to give you a call again the next couple of days, unless of course you have some real whales that need saving."

McDonalds must have some secret market research on their best customers that indicates Americans are getting fatter than ever now. After an alarming increase of stores that recently had unexpected, temporary closures, their investigation revealed it was due to a large number of their best customers getting stuck in the entrance door. At a pivotal moment like this, they knew they had to take action, and do it fast, to avoid this disastrous effect on in-store sales. You can't miss the new, large plastic box that all of a sudden appeared outside my local McDonald's entrance. They must have borrowed the idea from the airport terminals because the sign says "ATTENTION: If you cannot squoosh yourself into this box, you will not fit through the entrance. Please text your food order to #99 and an assistant will provide you with a baggage ticket. You can claim your order at the drive thru pick up window in a suitcase sized bag with a complimentary luggage cart."

6

—————————————

WAIT!!! I THINK I MIGHT HAVE LEFT MY DOGGY BAG IN THE AMBULANCE

TECHNICALLY, YOU REALLY don't fear death, but you'd have to admit you do wake up many a night in a cold sweat when you think "Dear God, what if I were to go into cardiac arrest and die just as the waiter delivered my order tomorrow? What would happen to that food?!?" That's when you finally got serious about your health and now make a Last Will & Testament you sign and give to your waiter with instructions on which lucky customer you're bequeathing your leftovers to if you happen to croak while you're eating.

Based on your predatorial eating habits, there's a very good chance your last words will likely be something like "I can't believe I ate the whole thing… are you sure there isn't anything left?"

When you asked your doctor if he could give you something to take the edge off the severe, adverse reaction

79

you were having with your diet plan, he told you he wasn't allowed to prescribe opioids for hunger pains.

There's a good chance your last words will be to the Grim Reaper when you say, "Whoa… unbelievable. It's really you?…. Wasn't expecting to see you so soon. Anyway, I'm sure you're probably on a tight schedule, but can you do me a favor and give me a minute to finish this burger and fries first?"

One of the unfortunate aspects of being obese is even if you have an impressive statement prepared for your immortal last words the odds are in favor of you being caught off guard when it happens. That's why, shortly before your overworked heart beats its last drumbeat, it's much more likely your last words will be something like "That's correct, dammit. You heard it right the first time. Is there some type of McDonald's policy restriction that says I'm required to have other people in the car with me when I order supersized, combo meals 1 through 5 at the drive thru? Are you worried I could eat myself to death if I ate all of this at one time? Don't be ridiculous."

When regular customers can't help but notice that a tubbo's face is turning blue at an All U Can Eat buffet, they know to be cautious about providing life-saving assistance right away. What they're hesitant about is if it would be rude to rush to give you, a record-setting buffet eating champion, the Heimlich maneuver, only to discover you were about to break the all-time Golden Corral eating record. That's why, understandably, no one dared interrupting you while you were catching your last breath before swallowing your last slice of pie for the record and for the coroner's report.

You can tell by their snooty looks that EMT's are secretly disgusted with people your size when they're called for a potential heart attack at an all you can eat buffet. They don't realize the contempt you have for them too. They never let you 'bend the rules' a little before you flatline by allowing you to scoop up your leftovers and bring a doggy bag in the ambulance in the unlikely case you survive.

When you showed up for your annual physical this year, your humbled doctor told you "I'm pleased, but I have to admit, very surprised to see you again.", so you greeted him with a cocky smirk. You took the low road because he's the one who lectured you last year in a disgusted tone by saying "If you're eating is so out of control you even brought a bucket of Kentucky Fried Chicken to a doctor's appointment, I'm bound by the code of ethics of my profession to inform you you'll probably be dead in a month, 3 months tops." That's why, before he started your exam this year, you asked him "Before we start, can I interest you in a drumstick?"

When the 911 EMT's came to save your life – again - to avoid having you file a complaint before they cleared the airway, they cleared the mouth, place that in a doggy bag, and then cleared the airway to get you breathing again.

Remember back when Fitbits first came out and every chubby person you know would constantly offer unsolicited updates to brag how many steps they had walked so far that day? If you remember that, do you recall any time recently that you've received an update from any of these people raving about their amazing stepping achievements? No? Of course not. These are the same people who excitedly make unsolicited announcements about every ounce they've lost when they first start their latest gimmicky diet, who mysteriously go dark on updates after 4 weeks tops. I'm afraid the Fitbits have all met the same fate of professional dieter's bathroom scales that became bearers of bad news: smashed to smithereens after the day it ratted you out as a couch blob for only walking 8 steps for the day.

With all the strength you had left, you stretched out your arms and legs and refused to budge as the EMT's tried to get you in the ambulance at the Waffle House parking lot after your heart attack. You finally relented when your waiter brought your doggy bag along for the ride so you'd have something to munch on at the hospital, if somehow you miraculously survived.

The EMT's called in backups when they found you choking at the restaurant and then 4 of them, and an innocent bystander Boy Scout, were finally able to join arm in arm around you to successfully give you the Heimlich maneuver so you could finish your lunch.

At the emergency room, as soon as you found out it was just acid reflux and not a heart attack, you asked your nurse if she could tell the pizza delivery guy waiting in the hallway that it was okay for him to come in now.

You were on life support once and your condition was so serious you could only be spoon fed 3 McDonald's Happy meals a day while you were in a coma.

You think modern EMT's have become pathetic weaklings because it took 8 of these wimps to lift you onto a gurney.

Your doctor denied your most recent request for a liposuction procedure because he said their rule is you have to wait at least 72 hours before the next one.

When the EMT's rushed you from the restaurant and into the ambulance and then had to use the defibrillator plungers to shock your heart to start beating again, the first thing you said when you regained consciousness was "Oh my God, I thought I was a goner there for a minute!....Did any of you happen to grab my doggy bag on the way out?"

When you came out of a coma one time, the first thing that you asked was "How long was I in a coma?". When the doctor answered "7 days", you shuddered with the terrifying thought of "My God! You're telling me I missed my last 70 meals?!? Someone get me a take-out menu before I go into a coma again!"

You were in a coma for 3 weeks one time and still somehow gained weight.

You went into shock one time from a blood transfusion. The blood type was correct but the cholesterol level was about 400 points below your usual level. Thankfully a quick-thinking nurse hooked up an eggnog intravenous without a moment to spare to keep you from flatlining.

Every boy in the Boy Scout troop earned a lifesaving badge when they all joined hands so they could reach far enough around to give you the Heimlich maneuver when you were choking at the Shoney's burger bar.

Other concerned diners called 911 because they thought you were choking but you ate so much you were actually just full to the top of your throat.

One of your biggest fears now is having a heart attack right in the middle of a huge feast. To prepare for that probability, you've begun the precautionary practice of keeping a sandwich in your shirt pocket to celebrate with if the EMT's are successful with their CPR attempts.

When you were on your death bed one time and things were looking bleak as you were drifting in and out of consciousness, nothing was more comforting to you than having your loved ones there. At the same time though, nothing was more irritating in this dire predicament than trying to say something when you just couldn't find the words. As you mumbled, your loved ones became confused and started arguing "I think he's trying to say something. Do you think he's trying to say his last words?!?" That's when your wife piped in and said "Nahhh…he's just chewing in his sleep. He does that all the time when he oversleeps and is more than 10 minutes late for breakfast."

Your ER doctor saved your life when, as a last resort, he ordered a Grubhub Burger King IV delivery to your emergency room bed when you started to go into convulsions from the fat free intravenous.

Unlike 99% of the people who come out of a coma after 6 weeks, instead of asking "Where am I?" like a normal person you asked "Soooo…what's for lunch?".

You've never been into personal fitness programs, but you're actually getting into better shape now that you've practically been forced into doing 30 minutes of cardio a day by trying on outfits in your closet until you find something that fits.

Whenever store clerks see you in the Running section of Dick's Sporting Goods, they always say the same thing "You look really lost, buddy. The Sumo wrestling gear is in aisle 5."

The only exercise you get is your involuntary belly dances after sneezes while you're employing your anti-jiggling techniques.

When you do an exercise walk, you like to maintain a certain cardiovascular pace, which most geologist observers would describe as a glacial pace.

At the gym you've gone to for the last 10 years, the receptionist always hands you a new membership application every time you visit.

You realize now you were probably overly ambitious when you thought you would start a cardiovascular exercise program to lose weight. After many failed attempts to go jogging, the best you were capable of doing was to go jiggling.

Your doctor has to wear a Vaseline lubed scuba suit to complete your prostate exam.

An EMT gave you mouth-to-mouth one time when you were unresponsive and ended up choking on the half of a Big Mac you were choking on.

When people ask if you've been working out, as you start to answer awkwardly, they can't help giggling before they say "Duhhh… Lighten up a little buddy, would ya'?. Can't you see that I'm just messing with you?"

Whenever old friends tell you "Wow! You look great. Have you been working out lately?" you immediately become very suspicious and start thinking "This must be one hell of a favor they're about to ask me about next."

When people ask if you've been working out, instead of replying in shocked disbelief, you hold up 2 fingers and ask "How many fingers am I holding up?"

People are stunned when someone your size tells them you do about an hour of cardio a day. Although it's technically true, you don't mention that all of your fitness training involves achieving your training heart rate while washing your hands before your 8 meals and with rapid 'hand to mouth' aerobic eating exercises.

People stare at you in utter disbelief when you tell them that you've been doing an hour of cardio a day for years. That's why you don't bother mentioning the elevator is broken at your building and that's how long it takes you to climb the 12 steps to your 2nd floor apartment.

After years of nagging her about getting into shape, you were psyched when you finally tricked your wife into joining a gym class. Boy did that strategy backfire. I admit I had no idea how much the fitness centers had been forced to cater to the needs of our rapidly growing obese American class these days. After a month of working out, I was shocked she was 10 pounds heavier than when she started. When I asked her how in the world that happened, she told me "My trainer told me she thought if I was willing to gain just 20 more pounds, I could compete on our new American women's Olympic Sumo wrestling team. Isn't that exciting? Can you imagine, me, of all people, a world-famous professional wrestler!" The worst thing about this was there's no denying she has a gift for this sport. The first time I asked her if we could discuss this like two grown adults, with hardly any effort, she belly bumped me into the back yard from the kitchen.

Your wife threw out your favorite, 'pigging out' salad spoon and replaced it with an hors d'oeuvres fork at meals. She figured if you're not going to get any real exercise, this would definitely qualify as a cardio workout for a glutton like you.

You're so out of shape, you can reach your training heart rate now just by jogging your memory.

You've always been revolted by the thought of any type of regular exercise, but you've gotten so fat you can't prevent doing 15 minutes of cardiovascular belly dancing every time you sneeze now.

When you shock friends and family by telling them you've started working out, they secretly make bets on if you've started to train for an upcoming hot dog or pie eating contest.

In your type of fitness group, after everyone saw an ice cream truck flip over in the street in front of the gym, your trainer abruptly canceled spin class and instructed everyone "Class dismissed! Grab your salad spoon or whatever you can find and it's every man for himself!"

Your exasperated fitness coach was so frustrated trying to come up with an exercise program, the best idea he could recommend for someone as big as you was "Go on a morning walk each day and don't stop until you find someone your own size to pick on."

You joined a Weight Watcher's gym one time but quit in disgust when you learned they somehow overlooked the #1 sport obese people can still enjoy competing in: a Sumo wrestling class.

You had to quit your new year's resolution to start jogging after your local police were flooded with complaints from your neighbors. They warned you, if you didn't cease and desist immediately, they would have no choice but to refer you to Homeland security and be charged for a terroristic threat for attempting to incite a seismic event.

When your doctor went to do your prostate check, he was very alarmed at first about how enlarged it seemed until he realized he was poking a pillow that was missing from your neighbor's couch.

Your doctor looks more like he's delivering a breached calf when he's doing your annual prostate exam.

You were too fat for the EMT's to find a pulse in one of the usually reliable places when you called 911 so they put 2 fingers to your jaw to see if you were still chewing.

Your wise guy personal fitness coach who was timing your run on a stopwatch asked "Where in the world have you been? I thought you were going to be here an hour ago?", before letting you know you just set a new personal best 100-yard dash time.

At your gym, the security guards apologized profusely after they told a pizza delivery driver, who was holding a large, meat-lovers pizza, "You must be clueless, pal. Didn't you even read the sign out front? This is a gym. No one here would have ordered a pizza, you big dummy." They had to grovel for forgiveness after you interrupted and explained "Sorry for the confusion guys, but I ordered it... What can I say? I get bored when I'm in spin class and an afternoon snack helps me to pass the time."

Neighbors breathed a huge sigh of relief when they saw you waving as you jogged past their house for the first time ever. At first, they were scared out of their wits because they were sure it was an earthquake when their ceilings cracked, the whole house shook and all their dishes started breaking.

People always enjoy the pure irony when you tell them "Sorry, I've got to run", but then trudge away like a sloth.

After he walked into the exam room for my appointment, my doctor took one look at me and it was like his lifesaving training techniques from med school instantly kicked in as he sprang into action. I was just about to open my mouth to say "AAAHHH" when he pushed me back on the exam table, balled his hands into fists and started violently pounding on my chest and doing emergency CPR compressions until I said "Gee whiz Doc... can you hold on there for just a second? I know I always look like I'm about to have a heart attack, but, if you're done with what you were doing there, can you take a look at my ear? I made this appointment because I think I have an infection".

On your annual physical this year, the doctor filling in the exam form listed 'My best guess: planetary???' for the question 'Description of shape?'.

A proctologist's worst nightmare is that someone with a butt exactly like yours might actually exist.

You were so embarrassed about all his fruitless probing, you tried to help your doctor out by saying "warmer... warmer... colder..." as he poked his finger into 3 other false butt cracks before he found the right one for your prostate check.

It's butts like yours that have popularized the use of forearm waders for Proctologists.

You're worried because, after some very concerning results on your annual physical, your family doctor was so alarmed he referred you to a specialist at the Extra Mayo Clinic for further cholesterol testing.

You bragged to your wife that you haven't gained an ounce since your last physical but she knows you're dumb enough to believe that because the doctor's scale only goes up to 400.

You hate the taste of your daily prescription pill and can hardly swallow it each day without gagging. That's why, at this year's annual physical, you asked your family doctor if he thought it would be okay to take your cholesterol medicine with chocolate milk and a cookie.

Your doctor had to drive you to the circus to weigh you for your annual physical.

You were rushed in an ambulance to the ER one time with what you thought was a rare, life-threatening disorder. After running a battery of tests though, the doctor just diagnosed you as being hungry after you missed a meal for the first time in your life. He cured you almost instantly when he recommended "Sneak into the nurse's breakroom and eat all their stale, leftover donuts. You should be feeling fine in no time after that. Let this be a lesson to you though about what a close call this was and how reckless it was of you to think you could skip dinner just because you had a 4-hour lunch at Golden Corral."

When you told your family doctor that you were having trouble sleeping at night, instead of giving you an insomnia prescription, he recommended a liquid Happy Meal feeding tube. It worked so well, you sleep through the night now and no longer feel exhausted when you wake up from having to be up and down the stairs 10 times a night to grab a snack when you get hungry.

You know what most people must be thinking when they first meet you: I wouldn't want to be the poor bastard who has to give you a prostate exam with your physical every year.

When your doctor did your prostate check, he heard a strange 'meowing' noise he'd never experienced in all his years as a doctor. He was very concerned and thought he'd have to run more tests until you told him "I think you probably poked my wife's missing cat, considering that's where she usually finds him whenever he's lost and we've looked everywhere else. Somehow he sneaks his way in there while I'm watching TV on the couch and I don't even notice. I'm not telling you how to do your job, but if you dangle a mouse toy behind my butt crack that usually coaxes him to come out so you can finish your check-up."

Your doctor has no idea how much medicine to prescribe for someone your size so he consulted with a zookeeper to see how much of a dosage of penicillin they give to the elephants when they have sinus infections.

When your doctor asked you if it makes you feel guilty at all when you overeat, you had to ask him to explain what he meant since overeating is the main source of any joy in your life.

People are stunned when you tell them you weigh a fraction of the doctor's recommended body weight for your height, but the fraction is 96/32's.

After you called 911 when you thought you were having a heart attack, it took all the strength you had left to prepare a bag lunch while you were writhing in pain on the kitchen floor waiting for the EMT's in case there was a long wait at the ER.

Most guys have trouble sleeping the night before they know they're getting a prostate check. Your doctor is the one who has trouble sleeping the day before yours.

If truth be told, once you're facing death everyone would like their final words to be memorable for their wisdom and solemnity to comfort their loved ones. That rarely happens with America's big overeaters though. Surprisingly, hospital records show many of them make a remarkably similar last request of their loved ones: "If - by some miracle - I somehow pull through this, can you check the ambulance to see if I left my doggy bag in there?"

You're thinking about writing a fat guy tell-all of your heroic experience undergoing one of the greatest chal-lenges to your non-existent willpower when you were cruelly forced to fast for 12 hours before a blood test. At least that's what you told everyone in the clinic's waiting room when your Grubhub delivery arrived. As you were munching on an extra-large Domino's meat lover's pizza and a 24-ounce Wendy's Frosty, they told you "We're all hungry, but are you sure you should be eating that before your blood test?". Just to rub it in their face, you bragged "They already harpooned this great white whale! I had to eat here because I'm racing against the clock to catch up on 3 missed meals and a midnight snack before I pass out from hunger."

Americans are such fakers when it comes to practicing yoga. When successful, yoga completely suppresses disturbances of your mind and body and will allow you to sink into a deep meditative trance that frees you from the distractions of the physical world. In my yoga class, everybody always looks like they've achieved the ultimate meditation peace in their perfectly still and breathless lotus pose positions. Only I know they're all a bunch of hypocrites when they brag to each other about their thrilling out-of-body experience during class when nothing could have distracted them from nirvana. As the fat Buddha of the class, I know all I've got to do is rip one accidental Burger King fart and you wouldn't believe how fast the 'out-of-body' bodies are climbing over each other in a stampede to get to fresh air.

After hearing the apocalyptical results of my annual physical and blood test from my doctor this year, I put my face in my hands and just sat in his office in stunned silence for a minute. Despite the doomed picture he had painted in excruciating detail, I couldn't resist poten-tially exposing myself to even greater misery. I just had to know one answer that would determine whether life was worth living anymore. I summoned my courage and then asked in a quivering voice "Doc, you gotta' tell it to me straight. Even though I might seem a little emotional right now after your devastating news, I just need to know one thing: would it be okay with you and my triglycerides if I agree to pour a little nitroglycerin in my beers when I eat my Arby's curly cheese fries?"

You always have good intentions to take up jogging after you become scared half to death about your annual physical results, but it never seems to work out. If people would just leave you alone you might have had a fighting chance to get into a routine, but they never do. When Good Samaritans see your beet red face and all the panting, wheezing and gasping you're doing they always assume you need CPR or an ambulance. After you thank them for their concern and then shoo them away after explaining you're actually just getting some exercise, you finally get back to your jog. 15 minutes later, when you're uncomfortably far from home and now think you're having an actual medical emergency, of course no help can be found anywhere in sight. With no other options available, you embarrass yourself by calling an Uber to get a ride home. Your humiliation is complete when you tell the driver the reason you needed a ride and he giggles uncontrollably the entire ride back when you tell him "It's the 6th house on the left." After an annual ordeal like that, it's no wonder you only jog once a year after your physical results are in.

You're sick and tired of your lifelong doctor getting all emotional when he finishes your annual physical exam each year. I can tell he at least attempts to keep it together and maintain his professional composure until

I leave. When I ask him how my results were though, he always just falls apart. His office scale only goes up to 375, so I know that couldn't be his concern. He gives me such a pathetic, tearjerker farewell though, it makes me curious if I did worse than last year's 200/160 blood pressure reading or finally broke into the 600's on my cholesterol level. I get so irritated about his complete loss of professionalism, I usually leave without finding out. I never leave though before taking the opportunity to say "See you same time next year, doc.", just to see him completely lose it while I pick up my jacket and Burger King take-out bag and leave.

When you turn 40 and you're an oxygen thieving couch blob, never bring a cheesesteak hoagie and milkshake to your annual physical. Your fitness fanatic doctor is bound to get pissed and ask why you brought these to your appointment. When you tell him "If you don't mind if I eat while you're playing with my prostate, they're my reward for fasting for 10 hours before you took my blood samples.", you should know this means war. For the next hour, he'll perform every health check he can think of to try to find some diagnosis he can scare the crap out of you with. When he finishes and is clearly flustered that he couldn't find a single thing wrong with you, don't dare get cocky as you're polishing off your milkshake and say "You look a little flustered there Doc. If you're worried I'm not going to pay the bill because you couldn't find anything wrong, don't you worry about that. I know how hard you tried." At that point you just guaranteed, against all the ethical principles of his oath, you're about to get an extremely rare "6 months to live if you don't lose 30 pounds" diagnosis out of pure spite. The kicker is, for the fake weight loss sugar pills he just prescribed, he tells you "Oh, by the way, you absolutely cannot take these pills with beer because one of the side effects, in rare cases, is a horrible death from spontaneous combustion. Just sayin'."

7

———————————————

FEAR OF FLYING BETWEEN FATSOES PHOBIA

WHENEVER I HAVE a middle seat on a domestic flight in America, I actually appreciate when my face smells like BO after it's been smooshed into the sweaty armpit of my World Champion Hot Dog Eating contest champion seatmate for the last 3 hours. I'm sure that sounds more than a little odd, but I'm lucky enough to have had a similar experience to compare this to. 10 to 1, I prefer heading into an important business meeting smelling like someone else's BO instead of their butt crack sweat.

You can tell the overweight Americans' lobby is rapidly gaining influence over congress concerning the airlines' perspective on the rights of fat people. I was shocked on my last flight when the guy in the window seat asked if I wouldn't mind passing his bedpan to the new candy striper on the aircrew staff. Who knew, but the airlines seem to be in agreement that, for at least 40% of their passengers, it would be harder for a camel to pass through the eye of a needle than for any of them to fit their fat asses into the airplane bathroom.

When the fat lady who just plopped into the seat next to you on the plane asks "Do you have enough room?" and shortly afterwards says "……Sorry, I didn't quite catch what you said…" It was because your response was muffled as you were gasping for breath due to the extent her right butt cheek was obstructing your airway.

From the way you were wheezing, panting, gasping and hyperventilating after your marathon endurance walk to the last row of the plane, your airplane seatmates had no idea how their oxygen masks didn't fall out before they passed out.

Even though you felt just fine, you were embarrassed that your belly was grumbling and making weird noises the entire flight and hoped no one could hear it besides you. After the plane landed though, you couldn't imagine how happy you were to discover there was nothing wrong with you, it was just your terrified seatmate who had been yelling for help beneath your belly the entire time.

Even avowed atheists look to the heavens and pour out tearful praises to God as you trudge by their row looking for your seat on the plane.

Even though you think you're practicing good manners, it's really a moot point for someone your size to ever ask your airplane seatmate if he has enough room after you've taken your seat. You might be oblivious to his situation when you keep asking "What? Huhhhh? I'm sorry I didn't quite get that. My hearing must be starting to go. Would you mind repeating that?". The only way you can make out what he's saying is when he makes a Herculean effort with the last ounce of strength he has and lifts your armpit flap that's draped over his head and yells "Hell no, I don't have enough room at all!!!", just before he passed out.

If oxygen masks keep dropping down as you squish your way down the airplane aisle.

The biblical metaphor about the impossible difficulty of a camel passing through the eye of a needle seems like a piece of cake to resolve compared to you trying to squeeze into the airplane bathroom.

There's really no need to act like you're being considerate by asking your airplane seatmate if he has enough room if his oxygen mask dropped out of the overhead compartment as soon as you sat down.

After you get settled in your seat on the plane, you always act like you're being considerate when you ask your seatmate "Do you have enough room?". For you though it's only so you can stop sucking in your belly if he tries to be polite by lying and says "No problem. I've got plenty of room here." when his scrunched-up face is already smooshed against the window.

You don't know how to find the words to explain to your airplane seatmate that you don't fit in the bathroom and hate to ask if he wouldn't mind emptying your bladder bag on his next trip. As if that wasn't bad enough news, you have no choice but to make him aware he only has the next 5 minutes to decide if he will pitch in to help to avoid a 'major accident', if he knows what you're saying. You also know it's extremely important for you to find the exact, right words of calm to broach this sensitive sub-ject. That's because, when you didn't say the right words on your last flight, your seatmate freaked out so bad the pilot had to make an emergency landing.

The flight attendant was forced to answer a question during her pre-flight safety briefing when the frightened passenger next to you raised her hand. After some whis-pering back and forth between them, she announced, "This is just a hypothetical example but, in the event of an evacuation, if any of you are sitting next to what you would guesstimate is a 400+ pound passenger, it's rec-ommended you climb over him instead of trying to go around if he gave you a forewarning when you sat down that he isn't planning to leave his seat in the event of an emergency evacuation until the complimentary snack cart reaches your row."

The full body search guys at the TSA, proctologists and rookie doctor prostate checkers all have the same recurring, worst nightmare: that someone with an ass your size might actually exist.

As a fat guy, you know you make your seatmates nervous when they see you stop at their row. That's why, whenever you take your seat on the plane, you're always friendly and courteous enough to tell the guy next to you, "It might be a good idea for you to flick your lighter under the vent to release your oxygen mask soon if you don't think you can hold your breath for the duration of the flight. I'm not bragging, but I just won first place in the Annual Texas Hot Chili eating contest so this flight is going to put you to the sniff test like never before."

You thought the guy next to you on the plane had a speech impediment, but it turned out his voice just sounded kind of funny only because he had trouble talking with your belly smooshed against his head.

When you take your seat on the plane, you hate getting yourself into awkward situations so you always introduce yourself immediately with the icebreaker "Excuse me, I'm 34B, the middle seat guy. Crappy break, huh?... Anyhoo, when you're done reviewing the plane evacuation pamphlet, I have a suffocation avoidance pamphlet of my own here I recommend you read from cover to cover. It's proven to be extremely helpful to previous seatmates of mine as their breathing becomes labored from the loss of oxygen.....So, now that we've got that awkward subject out of the way, are you flying for business or pleasure?"

You know you're overweight when you take up some of the seat of the person sitting next to you on the plane. You'll know you're in a special class of overweight Americans if you take up part of the seat of the person in the window seat across the aisle.

You would love to be able to take a really deep breath to calm your nerves like you used to as you took your seat on a plane. Ever since you gained a ton of weight though, it's just not worth risking anymore. For the fleeting moment of pleasure it provides, it's too embarrassing when everyone points a finger and blames you for the late take-off because you're the reason all the oxygen masks dropped down from the overhead compartment.

When you're as big as you are, you learn that you can't expect to ever have a moment alone in an airport terminal because of all the rude Americans with no manners. Terrified passengers never seem to mind intruding on your privacy and keep coming up to you before loading to nervously ask what seat you're in. Once they find out, they make such a commotion by sobbing inconsolably or hysterically laughing with relief that you can't get one moment of peace to eat the 6 chili dogs you bought to avoid passing out from hunger during the 45-minute flight.

There's no need for you to ask your airplane seatmate if he has enough room if his response is muffled by your stomach when he answers.

You know it's got to be a living hell for the people who are your unlucky seatmates on a plane, so, no matter how much you've got to pee, you're considerate enough to never get up to use the bathroom until they pass out from oxygen deprivation.

You thought it was odd how you felt fine but kept hearing a grumbling from your stomach the entire flight. Once you landed, you realized it was just your smothered seatmate calling for help beneath your belly overhang. Thankfully it stopped halfway through the flight when he must have passed out from asphyxiation.

You've caused an emergency landing by trying to 'sneak by' a dozing seatmate to use the bathroom on your plane.

You never saw 90-year-old ladies move like track stars as the time you had the window seat on the plane and calmly said "I'm sorry ladies, but I'm going to need to use the bathroom soon... and I mean 'very soon'."

Flying domestic in America these days in a middle seat must be a lot like what it's like for an unsuspecting Sumo wrestler referee to accidentally get stuck between the bellies of 2 combatants when the snack cart arrives at your row.

Remember the scene where the Ghostbusters got slimed by the junk food eating ghosts? That's how I usually feel when I get off a plane these days after spending 3 hours in my usual middle seat between 2 American style Jabba the Hutt twins. In my case though, I'd gladly prefer being submerged in whatever type of green, sticky, sewage slime it was that came from the ghost compared to the armpit or, even worse, butt crack slime I'm covered with.

You're obese, but surprisingly still love flying. For you there's just no place like an airplane where ginormous people get treated with so much respect. When you fly, people who would normally poke fun at you because you're so fat now cower in utter fear when they see you board their plane. No one is immune to the fear you instill in people as you leisurely squish and squash your way down the aisle. From years of practice, you know you're able to smoosh an entire row's faces against the window with one pre-planned fake sneeze. Of all the freaked-out passengers you see, the most terrified are the skinny ones with an empty middle seat next to them. Your ultimate dream of revenge is to cruelly pause for a moment at their rows with an empty seat and say "Excuse me… this must be my seat" and then chuckle to yourself as you pass after they feinted from shock. That's why it's a little-known secret that everyone just assumes all of us fatsoes are being discriminated against because we're always seated at the back of the plane. That's a complete falsehood. The secret is we actually requested seats like 72B and even paid extra because of the pure joy we experience from our conqueror's Squish, Squeeze and Smudge victory march past our groveling, conquered minions to get there.

Whenever you get on a plane, you quickly take your seat and then pretend you're asleep to avoid attracting any unnecessary attention to yourself. This is not your first rodeo though and as you take a peek around to see what's going on, other passengers are glaring at you because they assume you're at fault for the delayed take-off. Soon after, when you first hear the crackling of the intercom, you can almost mouth the words of the captain when he makes the unscheduled announcement "Welcome aboard and thank you for choosing United. Sorry for the minor delay, but we just completed our pre-flight safety check and it appears we'll have to balance our cabin weight before we're able to take off. It's nothing to be alarmed about, but the FAA won't allow us to take off if either wing is touching the ground. The good news is there's a simple fix to get us ready for take-off. If everyone on the left side of the plane, except 27C would grab their luggage and find an available seat on the right side of the plane, we think that should fix it and we'll be taking off into the wild blue yonder in no time. Thank you for your attention to this matter."

The problem with all the laws they enact in America is, after all the lobbying back and forth, the original problem that everyone knows is the problem doesn't exactly get addressed when bills are signed into law. Consider the recent laws that were passed that were called "The Bill of Rights for Airplane Passengers" for example. To their credit, they did add some conveniences to limit tarmac wait times, give ticket refunds and provide food and beverage reimbursements during excessive delays. The "crimes against humanity" abuses of the 800-pound gorillas on the plane were mysteriously left out though. Apparently, their PAC lobbied successfully to leave out criminal charges for excessive smooshing and squooshing in their seats and only made it a jaywalking level of misdemeanor for squeezing and squashing in the aisle. All this did was convince all the brazen tubbos that they basically have fat guy diplomatic immunity as plane passengers. It's gotten so bad, on my last flight you wouldn't believe what happened when they discontinued in-flight snack service because they ran out. When the tubbos heard the announcement, they decided to exercise their own rights and made such a ruckus having a massive water balloon fight with their bladder bags that the captain had to make an emergency landing to pick up more snacks.

They say that a lot of combat soldiers find God in a foxhole after they are miraculously saved when they didn't think they had a chance. That's why I think I have an all-time great suggestion for Jehovah's Witness recruiters. Instead of spending countless hours with their timeworn, highly ineffective, 'door to door' recruiting method, they need to put their recruiters on planes if they ever want to fill the churches again. There's never been a time when passengers don't have a pleasantly pleased expression

when the plane door is about to be closed and there's
still an empty seat between them. That carefree look of
good fortune disappears when they suddenly feel the
plane tilt as a profusely sweating human land mass of
strikingly disproportionate dimensions begins to squeeze
his way down the aisle. The closer he comes, the more
these faces of fear know what the combat soldier felt
when he was surrounded and had lost all hope. When he
pauses at their row and they're about to go into shock
from the fright, he double checks the row number and
then continues his trudge down the aisle. Beyond the
shadow of a doubt, this miraculous moment is the best
opportunity for the recruiter to hand both of these panting, ecstatic, non-believer passengers a pamphlet that
explains who arranged for them to dodge that bullet.
After visiting all those passengers, the best conversion
candidate is actually the guy who won the lottery ticket
of having the tubbo as his seatmate. Not only does the
Jehovah's Witness recruiter have a captive audience
peeking out between 2 bellies for the next 3 hours, but
he can make a convincing case that if this passenger
thinks this is a living hell, there's a worse one waiting for
him if his oxygen mask doesn't drop out of the overhead
compartment soon.

A lot of psychologists have been mistakenly diagnosing
American passengers with a "fear of flying" disorder. For
the fat ones who vow they will never fly again, nothing
could be further from the truth. Most plump American
plane passengers I've observed embody the courageous
spirit our World War II bomber command displayed
on rough flights that gained them the admiration of

the world's air forces. When they're on a flight and oxygen masks are popping out from overhead compartments, the wings are violently dipping up and down erratically, the plane is plummeting hundreds of feet per second, we're taking heavy flak and the frightened pilot announces over the intercom "We're all gonna' die!!! Flight attendants: secure the cabin for a crash landing!", none of the overweight American passengers even bat an eye while everyone else is losing it. When a flight attendant follows the captain with this second announcement though: "Due to all the turbulence and the crash you just heard about, we're sorry that in-flight snack service will need to be discontinued", that's when all hell breaks loose for the desperate tubbo passengers who face the stark truth that they might pass out from hunger and then won't know if they survived the crash.

You know it's going to be a really bad flight when you fall fast asleep as the plane is taxiing toward the runway and, 5 minutes after take-off, you wake up in a fright thinking you must have accidentally pee'd your pants. As you collect yourself, you breathe a huge sigh of relief when you realize you didn't pee your pants after all. You only thought you did because of the warm sensation you felt in your groin area from the bladder bag your seatmate snuck on your lap while you were sleeping. Now that he's sleeping peacefully and the bag looks like it's about to explode, you weigh your equally bad options: you either take a walk of shame down the aisle as everyone rears back in horror as they see what you're carrying or pull the latch on the emergency door. To avoid creating an inconvenience for your fellow passengers, you selflessly decide on the walk of shame option. As you arrive at the bathrooms though, just when you thought it was over, there's a long wait because 2 fat guys are stuck in the bathroom. At that point, all you can do as people give you disgusted looks is tell them "I know what this looks like, but you've got to believe me I'm only carrying this for a friend."

When you're five feet tall and sitting in the middle seat 38B between humongous male and female seatmates, it's understandable how the flight attendant missed you during her final headcount. Other curious passengers only knew you were there because every few minutes they could see part of your face poking out from between their conjoined bellies when you surfaced for air. When the plane landed and your seatmates left, the flight attendant was horrified and noticed you were sitting there and that your clothes and hair were soaking wet. Sounding desperate, she told you "I could lose my job if the captain finds out I missed you on the flight report. This probably sounds ridiculous, but I already talked to the cockpit to tell them you might need medical attention after 2 Sumo wrestlers somehow must have given birth by fission and then abandoned you and you're still drenched with amniotic fluid. I can't believe those dummies bought that. Can you do me a huge favor and back up my story so I don't get fired?" At a time like this, what else is a little guy supposed to say other than "I guess. The same thing happened on my connector, so I haven't had the chance to change yet anyway."

You know the quality of your flying experience is about to nosedive precipitously as your hope is shattered right before take-off when someone showed up to occupy the middle seat. Matters only get worse as you start to cringe when, for the second time in your life, you hear "Golly! I've never seen such a puny airplane seat in all my life. Would you mind trying to scooch on over just a little bit so I can squeeze into my chair?" Scooching isn't a mathematical term that provides an exact measurement. On a plane, it generally implies making a superhuman effort to contort your body into an extremely tortured position so you can hand over any extra room it's humanly possible for you to surrender to the lard butt who should have been required to buy at least 2 seats. Unfortunately, in the long history of plane travel, no scooching attempt has ever provided adequate room for a row mate to be in compliance with airline seating rules when he's the size of a baby hippopotamus. Consequently, for him to buckle his seatbelt so the plane can take off, all the other upset passengers are pissed off waiting for you to select which one you'd like to hold in your lap for the entire flight: his bladder bag or left man boob.

This could only happen in America. I actually discovered something more humiliating than sitting between two 400-pound Big Mac's on a death-defying 3-hour flight while practicing my Lamaze breathing techniques whenever I was able to surface between their bellies. I don't know how 43C contorted all that beef to be able to sit in one chair, but, as he settled in, the glacial latitudinal creep of his belly flaps eventually indented my face into 43A's belly. To make matters worse, 43A was wearing a tank top that failed abysmally to contain his 43D cup man boobs. As passenger after passenger paused at our row to take selfies with me and 43A in the background, I was horrified when I realized it must have looked like I was breast-feeding from a lumberjack mom from Bulgaria. That wasn't the worst of it though. The worst was when we landed and my mom called me to let me know she had seen me on Instagram. She wanted to tell me it gave her a fond memory of when she was breast-feeding me. She also wanted to know if I was wriggling around so much because I wanted the bottle instead of the boob, because most of the 3 million views thought that's what I was doing.

Few life experiences are worse than getting uncomfortably hot on a 3-hour plane flight whenever you're bookended in the middle seat by 2 enormous blubber butts. It only gets worse when you start to feel droplets trickling slowly down your forehead and onto your nose that basically cause waterboarding torture for you because your arms are helplessly trapped beneath their 2 bellies. A terrifying thought comes to mind at a time like this and you begin hoping against hope that you probably just started perspiring from the heat. Otherwise, the only plausible cause is that it's arm pit or butt crack sweat from one of your row mates, which you're well aware is the likely reason based on all your prior, miserable experiences with middle seat water boarding torture.

It's a 6th sense, but I fly so much, I can always tell when I'm going to have a flight from hell when I've been re-booked, there is limited seating available and the terminal attendant tells me "I just noticed in the system you are a 10 million-mile Delta SkyMiles Gold Platinum Plus lifetime member. Thank you for being one of our most valued customers, sir. I know your lofty status usually allows you to fly in the cockpit, but there aren't any seats available there or in 1st class. We do apologize for the inconvenience and would like to offer you a complimentary non-alcoholic beverage of your choice and an extra bag of stale, tiny pretzels. The good news is, as one of our most valued customers, you are being offered the first choice of our available seating. If you have a preference, I have four available seats in 3rd class. Would you prefer being squished, squashed, smooshed or slimed?" As pathetic as it may sound, I've had plenty of experience with each option and know, without a shadow of doubt, being smooshed is by far the best choice.

On most of my domestic flights in America, after I've been smooshed, squooshed, slimed and disfigured for 3 hours, I try to compose myself after this criminal assault as I follow my hippopotamic seatmate off the plane. As if this ordeal would never end, it never fails the Guinness Book of World Records people greet him in the terminal with wild cheers and congratulations for breaking the record for the heaviest passenger ever on a Boeing 717. As I try to sneak past without getting noticed, someone in their staff always gets a curious look as if he's seen me before and says "Heh, you look really familiar. Are you his agent or something?" so I tell him "Nahhh… you probably recognize me because I was also sitting next to the guy who broke the record last week."

If you've never noticed this before, whenever you see a Smart car leaving a Burger King it never fails that the guy driving it always weighs at least 400 pounds. The other thing you'll notice is he's always alone, clearly because no one else could possibly fit. If you're with me so far, riddle me this: why is this same type of ginormous guy, who can't fit any passengers in a Smart car that is at least 5 times the size of his airplane seat, allowed to purchase one seat when he should only qualify for a one-seat cargo plane for an elephant? I guess I should stop wondering about stuff like this because I think it increases the probability of my day being ruined whenever I fly. Every time I've thought about this on a plane, it never fails that Burger King guy shows up and interrupts my revery by saying "I'm in 72B, little buddy. If you can kind of skooch on over as much as you can, I think I can fit a leg in there so I can get my seatbelt buckled for take-off. Don't tell me you weren't warned, but once that seatbelt sign goes off, it's going to be like every man for himself fighting for space in a Smart car, if you know what I'm saying." I didn't know what he was saying at the time, but, from my harrowing experience that day, I'm absolutely sure I know now why you never see more than one 400+ pound occupant in a Smart car at Burger King.

The more you fly the more you get a 6th sense of what the flight will be like when you see certain signs before departure that you've never seen before. That's why, soon after I nodded off while we were taxiing for take-off, somehow I just knew it was going to be an all-time horrible flight. When you're in a subconscious state on a plane and feel your humongous seat mate urgently poking you for some reason, it's never a good sign. I knew in an instant it wasn't when he said "Sorry to bother your nap there little buddy, but I'm having an embarrassing situation here and wonder if you wouldn't mind giving a brother a hand. I'd be eternally grateful if you would hold this bladder bag that looks like it's about to explode for a minute while I go empty my puke bag. I'm so embarrassed, but I had no idea these things aren't pee proof."

Like anyone else, of course I fear death, but for me it pales in comparison to sitting on a plane next to an empty seat as they announce they're about to close the gate. It never fails that all of a sudden a sweaty, tank-topped, 400+ pound sumo wrestler look-alike comes waddling down the aisle. At a moment like this, I shut my eyes and pray as no man has ever prayed before that my hope against hope is somehow he's not sitting next to me. The desperate prayers are always abruptly suspended though when he taps my shoulder and says "43B? I think that's me... Golly! Is it an optical illusion or are the seats are a lot smaller back here than up front? ...Say... would you mind trying to scooch over a little bit? This looks like it's going to be one heck of a tight squeeze." I can tell this moment is like what my 'Judgment Day' is going to be like when my appeal for a suspended sentence to Heaven's clemency board is denied and I know I'm doomed. I know this because of the prior knowledge I have from my last flight when I must have sat next to 43B's identical twin. The air-line's position is "an emergency on your part does not constitute one for us" and they don't agree you can selfishly open the emergency door when you're the only one who's about to have a life-threatening emergency. They're official position is, if you're so scared of asphyxiation, they're fairly confident your oxygen bag should drop down before you're about to die from suffocation, otherwise press the call button, that is, if you still have the strength.

Even though it happens every flight, you still struggle finding the right way to express your bio-break needs to your airplane seatmate. I mean how do you go about explaining to someone you just met that his leg is getting warm because you don't fit in the airplane bathroom so you have to wear a bladder bag? One thing you know from experience though is you don't have a lot of time to break the ice by mentioning it somehow. That's because the second thing you have to explain is you hope he doesn't mind helping out because it usually has to be emptied at least 4 times on a 3-hour flight. Once you've got that off your chest, you casually tell him "I'm sure you're still in a little bit of shock hearing all this and I know it's a big ask, so take your time deciding. For planning purposes though, I need to make you aware that you have about 2 minutes before the ticking pee time bomb, bladder bag explodes in your lap."

All the airlines charge you extra now for supposedly selecting a better seat than the one you were randomly assigned. The one thing that they won't provide as an option though, which happens to be the most important indicator of your post-flight well-being, is how much do

43A and 43C weigh and what are their seated circumferences. I could have a seat in first class, yet would gladly switch seats with the guy in the last row of the plane who sniffs everyone's turds and hears "WOULD SOMEONE GET ME SOME TOILET PAPER, PLEEEAAASSSE!!!'
the entire flight if I knew that. When you have been smooshed between the Squish and Squash twins on your last 5 flights, take my word for it that it's worth paying any price to avoid this experience. It's even worse for me now that I know what I'm up against. The first few flights I toughed it out and took it like a man. As my courage has waned, I just know I'm going to wimp out on the next flight when I can't take it anymore. Once I hold my lighter up to the vent to get my oxygen mask to fall before I suffocate, I know the entire plane is going to be mad at me, not my oxygen thieving seatmates, because we had to make an emergency landing.

I make it a point to never fall asleep anymore before take-off whenever I'm in a middle seat and there are empty seats on both sides of me. I made this decision because, whenever I had done this previously, my nap was always ruined by a gentle tap on my shoulder. As I drowsily opened my eyes to see what the disturbance was about, I usually heard something like "Heh there little buddy. We're the aisle and window. Sorry we're late but the chili contest we were in went into overtime between the two of us. People call me Squish and this is my twin brother they call Squash. Our real names are Ronald and Harold, but somehow we picked up these great nicknames when we started flying… anyhoo, do you have enough room? If you ever wondered where that expression "10 pounds of poop in a 5-pound bag" came from, just watch us trying to squeeze into these tiny seats….Heh… where are you going little buddy? Did I say something wrong?…." As I fled the scene, from past experiences I've learned you most likely won't even get arrested for pounding on the cockpit door and demanding they let you off the plane if you cry like a hysterical little girl and they can see you're having a genuine full-blown, anxiety attack. When you weigh your options between guys like Squish and Squash, sometimes it's worth risking Federal terrorism charges by throwing yourself at the mercy of the captain. In the best of times, when the conveyor belt is still in place, they'll void your boarding pass and let you fly in the 1st class cargo hold with the 5 or 6 other middle seat guys who were in your same predicament.

Sometimes when you're just minding your own business while you're sitting on the plane before takeoff, you get so irritated by your spineless, frantic seatmates whenever you're in the middle seat. It never fails that after you sit down, they start sweating profusely, then comes the gasping and wheezing and finally they start wriggling around in their chair desperately trying to eke out any extra room they can find. When they finally admit defeat, they get such a sad and lost look of desperation, you're almost happy when they pass out a few minutes later from oxygen deprivation. As an added bonus when this happens, you don't have to ask your usual embarrassing questions about which one wants to have your excess belly rest in his lap and which one gets to hold the bladder bag.

I'll dare to go where no man has gone before, but don't assume I'm courageous. It's only because when you're in a real bind and discover you don't fit in the airplane bathroom when you've really got to pee, you'd be amazed how necessity leads to innovation. Even though it was your great idea, it wouldn't have been possible if the understanding flight attendant hadn't agreed to make the announcement "Please stay in your seats and remain calm. If everyone – and I mean everyone - would kindly pass their empty water bottles to seat 44B we should be able to avoid having to make an emergency landing due to a biohazard incident. Thank you for your cooperation with this request and for flying with United. We do appreciate your business. For any inconvenience we may have caused, the captain has asked me to inform you you'll be credited 100 extra miles if you are an Advantage club member."

You would think it would be pure hell when you sit between 2 hippopotamic land masses on a plane, but there are some surprising advantages. First of all, for someone who hates all the constant noise on planes, Bose has nothing in noise canceling headphone engineering that compares to the deafening silence of having your ears encapsulated in big belly ear muffs. I'm also one of those frustrated types who can never sleep on long flights. This method isn't for everyone, but, a minute or two after being seated, while you're suffocating and then black out, a flight attendant always stops by when your oxygen mask falls down and fits it over your face while you're unconscious. When I wake up 4 hours later and one of my seatmates offers me a warm face towel to wipe the armpit slime off my face and head, I have to admit, for an insomniac, these are some of the best sleeps I've had in ages.

You know your humongous size always shocks your seatmate when he first sees you, so you try to be courteous to everyone in your row and empathize with their frightening predicament. For this reason, after you sit down and the flight attendant completes her in-flight safety briefing, it's the perfect moment to inform window seat guy of a few more safety precautions of your own when you tell him "Heh buddy…… I've got some potentially bad news that might concern you. Before you get all worked about it though, this isn't my first rodeo. Once this plane takes off and gravity causes my belly to encroach only God knows where, your natural reaction will be to hold your breath at first like you're about to drown in blubber. I can tell you from experience though it's just a panic reaction and there's no way in hell you're going to be able to hold your breath for the entire flight or you're going to pass out. Take my word for it there's no need to worry. I've never seen it take longer than 5 minutes for your oxygen mask to drop down after I take my seat. After that you should be just fine. If you're in 'la la' land by the time it drops – no worries – I put the mask on my seatmates all the time. Unless you have any questions, I'm going to go to sleep now. I hate to see people suffer, so – if you wouldn't mind – please wake me when it's over."

You always hate when the poor guy in the middle seat on your flight is bracketed by another guy who's just about your size, which is Super-Heavyweight Division Sumo Wrestler. It never fails that the competitor comes out in both of you after middle seat guy passes out from asphyxiation. Even though neither one of you has lifted a finger in years to exercise, somehow both of you discover a natural talent for Sumo wrestling moves. As if a referee blew a whistle to come out fighting, you instantly start to bump, parry, crotch grab, gut wrench and slime each other with butt crack sweat to win the leftover sandwich prize on the tray of middle seat guy who didn't get a chance to finish it before he passed out.

Without them saying anything, you can tell the airlines are all getting nervous about the epidemic of increasingly obese passengers on flights. On my last flight, I could tell there's a new silent movement going on to finally start fighting back. At my gate in the terminal, you couldn't help but notice there was a port o' potty next to the boarding area entrance. A sign next to it said "All passengers are required to stick your butt through the door before boarding. If the port o' potty sticks to your butt, there's no way in hell you're going to fit in the plane bathroom. If you don't have your own or need an extra, you're required to pay $89.99 for a bladder bag before you board. Thank you for your cooperation with this matter."

8

IF IT'S HUMANLY POSSIBLE, DID YOU SAVE SOME ROOM FOR DESSERT?

YOU RACKED YOUR brains about this, but the only plan you came up with that could possibly work for you to follow the doctor's strict orders to finally stop your dangerous habit of overeating at meals was to schedule more daily meals. So far, so good until I hear what he has to lecture me about at my next check-up.

You feel like you might just freakin' lose it the next time some well-intentioned stranger offers the usual unsolicited advice of "Heh buddy, it's none of my business, but you should really start thinking about watching what you eat." Little do these mushminds know that fat people already do watch what they eat more than any other people alive. For us, apparently, it's an unresolved self-control challenge that's our problem because we just don't watch it long enough before we devour it.

You're not one for avoiding confrontation in your life. You live by a courageous 'If it's in your way, eat it' rule only fat people would understand.

After you walked through the county fair, a farmer started asking everyone around "You wouldn't happen to have seen the side of beef I just had on the spit not 2 minutes ago? Darndest thing I ever saw. How in thee hell does a 600-pound ox just up and vanish like that?!?"

I've tried and tried to watch what I eat. The only progress I've ever made so far is to watch what I'm about to eat.

From the way you look, it sounds impossible to believe to people who ask, but you actually do watch what you eat. What you don't mention is your method is to evaluate your championship eating technique by watching videos of what you ate at all the eating contests you've entered.

Why should I watch what I eat when every time I sit down to eat lots of people do it for me. Wherever I go to eat, a crowd forms as they're all excitedly telling each other "Wait till you watch how much this tubbo can eat".

If you're watching what you eat and still can't lose any weight, your best bet is to watch it longer before you eat it.

When your wife wants to hide something from you in a place she's sure you'll never find it in a million years, she always puts it in the refrigerator vegetable drawer.

To salvage some self-respect, you changed your dog's name a year after you bought him because every time you told people his name was Scraps everyone started laughing hysterically.

When your dog stares at you with a look of love, admiration and a complete sense of trust, you can tell he has no idea he's just one big snowstorm away from being added to the meal plan if you can't make it to the McDonald's drive thru for more than a day.

Your wife doesn't buy the "I don't know how it keeps happening, but the new pet rabbit broke out of its cage and escaped just like the last 10 we've had." alibi you offer whenever she's more than 30 minutes late with the groceries.

When your wife gets home late from grocery shopping, she always has to go right back out to the pet store to buy new guppies for the aquarium before the kids notice.

People wonder what you mean when you say "I'm so hungry, I could eat another horse."

The only way your wife has been able to help you lose weight is when you tell her each day "I can't believe I ate the whole thing." and she replies "Yup… I never would have believed it either, but you definitely ate the whole thing." Her response only prompts you to become even more suspicious though so you usually ask the follow up question "So…uhhh… what's with the chain and lock on the refrigerator then if you've got nothing to hide?"

I tried one time to start watching what I eat at restaurants, but it was too much for me all at once. That's why I opted to start with baby steps by watching what other people weren't going to eat while I was eating. This method was so much easier to start with when you're trying to get your appetite under control and, as an added benefit, waiters will usually gladly give you doggy bags from the leftovers on other tables.

My wife complained to me one time that she didn't want to go out to eat with me anymore because she was always so embarrassed about how much I ate and how long she had to wait for me to finish. Since I love going out to eat, I ended up having to basically agree to an unconditional surrender. Our 'agreement' is I get to eat as much as I can eat in no more than 2 hours. After that, no matter what's left, however much I beg and plead, goes into doggy bags. I guess it was the best deal I could get under the circumstances, but there's nothing I hate more than having to rent a U Haul trailer for the doggy Hefty trash bags every time we go out to dinner now.

Even though you find it extremely insulting, your wife feels it's a necessary precaution to take her dog with her when she goes grocery shopping to prevent you from doing anything drastic if she was late getting back. This seems so ridiculous to you, you try to defend yourself, but the only pathetic excuse you can come up with is "Geesh, hon…Don't you think maybe you're taking this a little too far? I know I've eaten a turtle, 3 rabbits, 2 hamsters, a snake, a guinea pig and so many aquarium fish I can't even count them all, but you must have a low, low opinion of me to think I would ever eat our dog. Even if I knew I was near starvation, it would never cross my mind to think about eating a precious, little Poopadoodle… again."

When my wife brags to friends "I know he's gotten very heavy, but I'm watching him like a hawk now. I know everything - and I mean everything - he eats now." my guess is she's still only watching about 5% of what I eat at most.

At restaurants, kids are always gawking at you and asking their parents "Mom, can we stay a little while longer? Pleasssseeee? We want to see if the fat guy can really eat all that!"

People who are sitting at the tables near yours in restaurants post guards when they have to get up for a minute to use the bathroom.

My wife hates when we don't make a dinner reservation at a restaurant and then finds out there's a long wait when we get there. It's not that she doesn't enjoy a relaxing night out and having a few leisurely drinks at the bar before we eat. As usual, I'm the problem when we go out and I'm expected to wait 90 minutes to eat when I'm already hungry enough to eat a horse. The last time we waited, she couldn't take it any longer and warned me "I'm not staying if you keep doing that. How do you expect me to have a relaxing night out when I'm enjoying a glass of wine at the bar while you're embarrassing me by standing next to the exit offering $10 dollars to everyone who walks by for their doggy bag?"

You think the dumbest question a waitress could ever ask you is "Are you done with that?". Whenever you've been asked this before, your first reaction is to give a sarcastic response like "Well, Duhhh", but usually you decide on the kinder option and tell her "I'm guessing this is your first day on the job, ehhh?"

My wife hates going on romantic restaurant dates with me because she says I always 'ruin the ambiance' while I'm waiting for her to finish after I'm done eating by constantly asking diners at nearby tables "Excuse me, are you going to eat that?"

When you're on a romantic date at a restaurant, it's hard for you to focus on the conversation because you keep interrupting passing waiters to ask them for doggy bags of leftovers at other tables.

Your favorite waiter at the All U Can Eat diner you go to all the time will remind you sometimes when it looks like you're overindulging "Remember to leave some space for dessert." You always appreciate the reminder because you go measure how much room you have left to expand before you won't fit out the door anymore to help make your decision to have the Jello pudding or hot fudge sundae for dessert.

You never worry about checking expiration dates when you are grocery shopping since most of what you bought is gone by the time you get home anyway.

When you stop chewing and your regular waiter notices and gets very alarmed that something must be terribly wrong because he's never seen you act this way before, you tell him "Calm down. No need to call the EMT's. There's nothing to worry about here. I'm just taking a short break after breakfast before I go get some lunch."

When someone asks you "What's good on the menu?", there's always a dead silence in the busy restaurant as onlookers listen like it's Warren Buffet giving a stock tip.

The same waiter who asked "Will you be dining alone?" asked 2 hours later after you finished eating "Would you like ALL of this on one check?"

When you go out to eat with old friends, their secret, over/under bet on when you first say "What's a guy gotta' do to get something to eat around this joint?" is 30 seconds.

When you complain to your wise guy waiter that your order seems to be taking a long time, he tells you "I can check on it, but, if you don't mind my saying so, it looks like you've already had enough to eat." When you give him a confused look and say "But I haven't even been served anything yet", he says "Oh, I'm sorry, I didn't mean to confuse you. I meant in general."

People are always telling you at restaurants "Oooohhh boy, you don't look like you could eat another bite", before the waitress even brings any of your 6 plates of food.

At your favorite restaurant, the owner always visits every table to ask the customers if they enjoyed their meal. You cringe every time you see him coming when he says "Whoa ho! By the look of your big belly you must have really enjoyed your meal!" This always prompts you to say "Actually I haven't been served yet. Would you mind checking in the kitchen to see what's taking so long?"

Your wife was really mad at you the last time she went grocery shopping and told you "I'm warning you for the last time. You have to learn to control your panic response. You can't just start eating the kids' pets every time I get stuck in traffic on the way home from the grocery store".

Your wife put wheels on your kitchen table chair that keeps you from overeating now. With this ingenious idea, once your gut reaches maximum expansion, you're so far away from the table you can't reach your plate with your telescopic fork anymore. When you tried to stand up to eat the rest, somehow she calculated exactly that you wouldn't be able to move because your chair was stuck to your butt.

Whenever you go to the grocery store, concerned shoppers look at your train of shopping carts and then start checking for weather updates on their iPhones wondering if they missed the news about the snowstorm of the century.

You hate when people take a curious interest in you at a highway restroom as you're leaving a stall because you've heard the question you know they want to ask too many times before. That's why you go out of your way to beat them to it by saying "Hmmmm… let me guess: you were about to ask me 'How in the world are you able to wash your hands before returning to work like the sign says?'" Payback's a bitch though. The same guy who walked out of the bathroom chuckling cruelly with his young sons, feinted like a little girl 5 minutes later when you handed him his Big Mac and said "Figure it out yet?"

When you got in the checkout line, the cashier at your grocery store wondered why you'd be buying 10 empty boxes of cookies. Your only answer is "Duhhh. Do you think I would be if the guy in charge of security hadn't told me he's got video evidence of a shopeating crime if I should try to walk out without paying for them?"

Your grocery store's safety rules require you to hire a conductor to steer the front shopping cart of the 8 you have ratchet strapped together in your train.

Grocery store cashiers just sneer with contempt every time you try the "Oh, would you look at that, I must have accidentally grabbed an empty box of cookies. Let me just run back to aisle 9 to grab a full one."

You've never felt the need to check the expiration dates on your perishable purchases when your cashier bags your shopping cart full of wrappers.

The best thing about my wife having friends over for dinner is she doesn't want to make a big scene in front of them, like she usually does, complaining about me being a glutton. To avoid embarrassing herself in front of her friends, she'll walk into the kitchen and see wrappers all over the floor and say "What a mess. The *dog* must have been in the trash again."

When you first got cable, you kept your old satellite dish for spaghetti night.

After you asked your waiter for a doggy bag, he looked baffled when he took a quick glance at all your empty plates that had been licked clean, so you gave him a wink and pointed to the leftovers on the table next to you.

To feed you properly, your wife researches the FDA recommended daily calorie allowances and then multiplies her ingredients by 8 to prepare your meals.

You don't snack between meals anymore, but it's definitely not because you're on a health kick. You miss snacking terribly, but you eat so much at meals now there just isn't any time to anymore unless you gave up your 10-minute bathroom breaks between meals.

Your wife is trying to become a better cook, but it's because, after she's tried everything else, she believes it's the only way she could make you start fantasizing about her again.

You think it's cute how naïve your wife was when she started blindfolding you at the end of dinner before she hid the leftovers in a secret hiding spot she thought you would never find. Of course, that was before she realized you can track leftovers better than a bloodhound can track an escaped prisoner.

A lunch break to you is the break you take between your late morning and early afternoon snacks.

You eat so much when you have dinner at your mother's, sometimes you decide to just sit and wait another 20 minutes at the table after you're finally finished eating dinner for breakfast to be served.

When your family meals are placed on the table, it looks more like the July 4th Nathan's hot dog eating contest is just about to start.

Your wife is never certain if you're just trying to be polite when you act like you loved a surprise, new dinner meal by telling her "I absolutely loved your new recipe!". She loves to hear the compliments, but at the same time can't help but wonder "I know he said he loved it, but if he liked it as much as he said he did, why wouldn't he have eaten enough to split his pants or hit me in the eye with a shirt button like he usually does with his favorite meals if he wasn't just trying to avoid hurting my feelings?"

When it's too quiet at meetings, my boss uses that old cliche all the time "C'mon, don't be shy. There are no dumb questions." I've never told my wife about this though because she actually does ask unbelievably stupid questions. One of the all-time dumbest, which makes me cringe every time I hear it, is "You've already had 5 servings, are you sure you'd like another helping dear?"

Your wife tried everything, but finally gave up trying to convince you to stop overeating at meals. Instead of changing your mind, she secretly adds Benadryl now to her recipes for your dinners to make you fall asleep before your 4th helping to keep you from eating yourself to death.

Your wife is always warning the kids at dinnertime "If I told you once, I've told you a thousand times: stop feeding your father under the table."

When you tell people you're having leftovers for dinner, it's eerie to you that everyone you tell looks at you with stunned disbelief and then asks the same exact question "How could that be possible at your house?!?"

You always know when it's just about that time to stop eating and start thinking about what you'll have for dessert when you can no longer reach your plate with your fork.

You have no clue that when people ask you if you know the time, they mean something a little more specific than lunch, dinner or snack time.

Even though you get asked at least 20 to 30 times a week, you still think the dumbest question anyone could ever ask you is "Did you get enough to eat?"

Your wife pisses you off a lot of times before supper by telling you "Don't let me catch you snacking before dinner or you're going to ruin your appetite!". When it comes to eating though, you've told her many times before not to tell you what to do, so, to outsmart her, you put away the snacks and have a late, late 2nd lunch instead.

When a fat guy tells you "I honestly can't remember if I ate lunch. I guess I better eat something in case I didn't to avoid passing out from hunger before dinner.", you'd have to be one of the most gullible doofuses in history to sympathize with him when he tearfully confesses that his fatso amnesia must have reared its ugly head again.

You play a fat man's version of Russian roulette when you're anxiously waiting for your wife to get back from the grocery store and try to eat the cheese from the mouse traps without getting your tongue caught – again.

At the grocery store, you heard a woman asking about a food's expiration date but didn't look into what that meant any further because you figured there's no way anything you bought could spoil on the ride home.

The bumper sticker on your Smart car says "Leftovers are for wimps who can't handle their food".

Even though she brought home a carload of junk food just yesterday, your wife can always tell when there aren't any snacks left in the house again. When you go to greet her when she gets home from work, the telltale sign is if she noticed you have a mousetrap stuck to your tongue when you kissed her to say hello.

To stunned onlookers, you never look like you could eat another bite when you sit down for lunch at a diner and then you proceed to make fools out of all the dummies who assumed that.

Sometimes when I know I can't eat another bite of my dinner, I shock everyone by getting up from the table to take a 30 second break to regroup. After that breather, I never have a problem finishing off the rest of the food on my plate because somehow I've always been able to make room for leftovers.

You don't have too many inviolable principles but you often tell waiters, who just asked if you'd like a box for the leftovers, "I would gladly prefer an overeating death with dignity before I'd ever betray my sacred honor with the shame of asking for a doggy bag." Every waiter you've ever told this to is so shocked and at a loss for words from your unwavering determination and solemn vow, they usually blurt out something like "I'm so sorry. I had no idea finishing your meal was so important to you… Let me talk to the EMT's to see if they can wait a couple of minutes with the defibrillators… Do you think that would be enough time to finish up?"

You know you have an eating disorder when you have a fork with a telescopic handle that comes in handy when your belly is so full you can't reach your plate anymore.

When you can't take another bite, but your pride is telling you – as God is your witness - that you've never had leftovers before and over your dead body you won't today either, this is usually all the motivation you need to start swallowing the rest of it whole.

Most grocery store shoppers unload their shopping cart into their car. You take your cart of empty wrappers and boxes you just bought over to the dumpster as you leave the store.

I had no idea before my wife confessed to me one day that she doesn't like to go on romantic dates with me anymore because she's so embarrassed when I ask for doggy bags. When I tell astonished friends this, I'm forced to explain "Duhhh… not for me silly. Her prob-lem is, after I'm done quickly scarfing down my food, it's embarrassing that, while I wait for her to finish, I pass the time scanning the room with my binoculars. She says it's even more humiliating after that when I call waiters over to check on diners who don't look like they're going to finish their meals and then tip them if they'll ask 'All finished here? Would you like to box this up… for the guy over there who's staring at your plate through his binoculars?'".

If you had been at the Last Supper, the most important part of the gospel would have been written drastically different than the one we know. At the end of dinner, Jesus probably would have scanned around the table and then, hardly able to conceal his irritation, said some-thing like ' Geeeshh…who ate all the bread?!? I was just about to say something really important'.

Whenever your wife doesn't feel like having a lot of leftovers after Thanksgiving dinner, she always lets you clean up afterwards. This serves a dual purpose because whenever you're allowed the liberty to be left alone long enough with all the leftovers, you don't need to embar-rass your wife in front of her guests by eating out of the trash.

People like to ask you what your favorite junk foods are, as if they're making small talk. Secretly though, they're curious to find out so they can avoid having it do the horrifying things to them that they've clearly done to you.

All the fish in your aquarium suck in their stomachs and cram into the sunken ship when you stare at them lovingly with your "I could use a quick sardine snack to go with these cheese and crackers before dinner" look.

Even when you just had a wonderful bonding moment, no one who knows you well has ever been fooled into telling you "What's mine is yours" right before the waiter brings your meals.

It takes you so long to eat dinner at a neighbor's house, instead of offering you an after-dinner mint they offer you an after-dinner breakfast-bag-to-go instead.

You told your wife it's your doctor who's to blame for why you eat 6 meals a day now. She got all snooty with me and asked "How in the world could you think somehow he's to blame for your out-of-control gluttony?" So, I told her "He's the one who scared me half to death when he told me I'm going to die soon if I didn't stop snacking between meals. I gave that my best shot for a couple of hours and then thought 'who am I kidding?' That's when I came up with the miraculously, successful plan of replacing my snack breaks with extra meals. The weird thing is I don't even miss snacking now and I feel healthy as a hippopotamus!"

Technically I really don't fear death, but I would have to admit I wake up in a cold sweat a lot of nights thinking about it. In my worst nightmare, the horrifying scenario is always the same: the Grim Reaper shows up and tells me "Times up, fatso. Grab your hat, you're coming with me." just as the waiter was about to serve my food. Then I have a desolate moment that death might truly be awful when I ask "Mr. Reaper? Would it be okay if I took my meal in a 'To Go' bag?". He gives me a funny look and then tells me "Look pal, I don't know how to tell you this, but you won't be needing it where you're going." To get back to sleep, I try to convince myself over and over that this must mean there will be plenty to eat all the time wherever I'm going. It never works though because I fear the truth is I'm headed straight for a Weight Watchers Marine boot camp in purgatory to whip me into shape because there are maximum weight limits for rookie angels.

9

THE EXTRA-MAYO CLINIC DIET
FOR OVERWEIGHT AMERICANS

IF YOU'RE CONSIDERING starting a diet, but don't know when the time is right like you do with your Viagra, I can help you with that answer. At any point when your face cheeks start looking like ass cheeks or - even worse – people can see ass cheeks next to your face cheeks when you're sitting, it's definitely time to diet.

This might sound unbelievable, but your current diet allows you to order anything – and I mean anything - you want at the drive thru… just as long as you don't pick it up.

You think it may finally be time to begin researching for a diet after the last time you got out of a long, hot shower you noticed your feet were still dry.

You've gotten so fat, friends don't even have to ask how your diet is going anymore. They're able to take a look for themselves to see if you're making any progress based on how far below the bottom of your t-shirt they can see your belly button.

You hate how you have to be so sneaky around your wife whenever she quits a diet that has failed miserably. It almost feels like you're betraying her when you take daily, secret trips to the McDonald's drive thru and pig out in their parking lot. Before you drive home, you take a couple of slugs of Listerine and carefully make sure you've thrown out all your trash so she doesn't suspect a thing when you arrive. This probably sounds ridiculous, but it's definitely worth the effort when you consider the alternative. Once your wife starts secretly serving you her leftover diet food to see what effect it has on you, a revenge worse than death would surely await you if eating it caused you to lose 10 pounds when it made her gain 20.

As a married guy, you hate how you always feel compelled to start secretly cheating almost immediately for the good of the marriage when you're dieting together. To you, it's all part of being faithful to your loyalty vow by showing support for your wife's sarcastic opinion of "No one could lose weight on this ridiculous 'eat right and exercise' scam diet."

Your wife has been on so many diets since you got married, you can interpret what 8 different, wounded animal screams mean when she's standing on the bathroom scale.

To your wife, an unforgivable, irreconcilable difference now that could possibly threaten the survival of the marriage would be if you were ever dumb enough to lose weight on the same diet she gained 10 pounds on.

You're secretly flattered when co-workers can tell you're making progress on your diet when they make comments like "You must be doing fantastic on your diet. I'm sure I've never seen catsup stains so low on your tie before."

When your friends and family haven't seen you in a while they know it usually means you're spending a lot of time alone at home to finally get serious about losing weight. You call this solitude your 'panic dieting' stage. This option is usually decided on about the same time you came to the realization that there's no sense trying on clothes to see if anything fits if you can't even squeeze out your front door now.

You've always talked in your sleep, but your wife has told you it's gotten so bad while you're on a diet that she's going to have to put your phone in the safe till the morning. She doesn't know how you're doing it subconsciously, but your sleep is interrupted every night at 3am now when the Grubhub delivery driver rings the doorbell with your order.

Your weight fluctuates so much from all the gimmicky diets you're always on there are 8 different pants sizes in your closet and they all fit at some point every year.

In the worst Spring dieting years, you remember to leave the pool water level 3 feet lower than normal so your wife won't be humiliated by flooding the neighbor's basement again after she does her first cannon ball.

Your favorite time of the year comes between quitting your New Year's resolution to lose 20 pounds and the start of your Spring diet to lose 30 pounds. During this carefree interlude, you feel so liberated from all those guilty feelings about being overweight and watching what you eat, knowing you'll be pretending to do something about it again soon.

When your wife goes on a Spring diet, all experienced husbands know it's a good time for you to start practicing your convincing 'cool, calm and collected' reaction to the shocking announcements she'll be making in front of the bedroom mirror. If that sounds like an odd thing to work on, it doesn't to any married guy. From our annual experience, we know it's important to a wife's confidence to avoid looking like you're going into shock the first time she tells you "Well, it took a lot longer than I expected, but I guess I'm finally ready to start wearing a bikini again."

If you've heard it once, you've heard the dumbest question anyone has ever asked a thousand times which is "It seems impossible, but are you absolutely sure you're allowed to eat that on your diet?"

You are uniquely qualified to write a book titled "100 Fad Diets That are 100% Guaranteed to Make you Gain Weight or Your Money Back".

Your wife likes when you diet with her because it shows that you'll still support her crazy dreams even at some of the most challenging times in your relationship. What she absolutely loves though is that you always have the empathy to gain more weight than she does, which allows her to be the selfless one who quits before the diet can do any more damage to you.

You're always happy when your wife crashes off her latest diet, but it's mainly because she can't complain as much as she normally does about her unwanted weight while she's catching up on her chewing and swallowing.

You've heard it's important to be understanding as a husband, but you'll learn there's no 'How To' manual on being compassionate when it comes to diets. Luckily, I've always been able to tell when a diet announcement can

be expected soon from my wife. When I pay close attention, her butt always provides signs that are remarkably
similar to the phases of the moon that tell me all I need
to know. I first notice the weight gain has become a concern to her when I see the telltale sign of a clear 'waning
crescent' moon of butt crack exposure in her hip hugger
jeans. Soon after, the butt crack reveal has doubled in
size to the Waning Gibbous phase in the same jeans.
A few weeks later, when the original hint of butt crack
exposure now looks like a full-blown Harvest mooning, I
know the announcement is imminent when she tells me
"We need to talk" and I notice she's wearing a selection
from her Snuggie attire.

Diets have been so hopeless for you, you fired your dietician and became desperate enough to hire a magician to
see if he could come up with a trick to make it look like
most of your butt had disappeared.

Quitting junk food 'cold turkey' proved to be impossible
so you quit by using the 'cold fried turkey with a scoop
of mayo' method.

You get so fed up now when you hear your wife complaining about the failure of her latest fad diet, you
always end up telling her the same two things. You start
with "For once in your life, can you just forget all the
gimmicks and highly questionable, miracle diets and
simply try eating right and exercising for a while?" After
you tell her this, it never fails that almost immediately

afterwards you follow up by saying "I'm so sorry. I must have been out of my mind to say such crazy things. How could I have been so unfeeling to give you, my forever love, such ridiculous and impossible advice?...... Now, honey, would you please put down the gun?"

You know it's time for a diet when you go to Walmart to pick up a few things and are met by a swarming mob that look like paparazzi who are actually photographers looking for fresh faces for the 'People of Walmart' big butt Instagram pictures.

Your wife was furious with you after she asked if you noticed anything different about her lately and you failed the 'supportive husband' test by not realizing she'd already lost 12 ounces by the 6th week of her diet.

When you've had some puny successes on a diet as a typical American fat guy, you get unique compliments from neighbors like "I don't mean to be nosey, but have you lost weight? I don't want to be rude, but I've noticed recently we only experience partial eclipses now when you go past our house at sunrise on your morning walks."

The nutrition clinic told you the most important key to a new diet is to avoid planning to fail by setting impossible goals, which would make you even more dejected about your unwanted weight. You understood the great wisdom of this advice immediately so, when you set your

12-week diet goals, instead of losing 30 pounds your practical goal was to lose 30 ounces.

After failure upon failure of weight loss plans, to avoid looking completely incompetent your frustrated dietician recommended that you might try brushing your teeth for 5 minutes at a time, 30 times a day. When you asked him how in the world that was supposed to help you lose weight he said "I'm not saying it's failproof for a guy like you, but that's the last humane thing that I can think of that might lower your daily caloric intake. Otherwise, the last resort is to ask your wife to handcuff you behind your back before you wake up and stick duct tape over your mouth to see if that helps you cut down on snacking."

I conducted some secret mood experiment studies on my wife and concluded an astounding 90% of her bad moods are directly related to what stage she's reached on her most recent diet disaster. This might sound like a stunning breakthrough that could help cure her dark moods, but it turned out to be useless information I decided to keep to myself. It turns out, when you're a spineless coward, you would prefer walking barefoot over hot coals than potentially taking your life in your hands by sharing your diet observation findings with her.

You always eat today as if your crash diet starts tomorrow.

I'm sure women have a more scientific method, but, through trial and error, I've learned one of the most reliable methods for a guy to evaluate his butt reduction diet progress is timing how long it takes to sniff your farts after you hear them.

When your wife's latest diet failed you proudly told her that she's your greatest inspiration. When she gave you a confused look, you told her "I felt so alone and betrayed when you were on that stupid diet. Can't you see? The key to the happiness of our marriage is when we enjoy spending time together doing things that are fattening."

You take it as a compliment to all the sacrifices you've made with your years of constant dieting efforts when people ask "I don't want to embarrass you, but have you been dieting? I don't know exactly what it is, but up close you look a lot less humongous to me than you usually do."

When you and your wife say you're going on a New Year's diet no one can tell by the way you're pigging out by January 3rd whether you had a delayed start or already quit.

You gained so much weight on the South Beach diet, you had to preserve some self-respect by not quitting a bikini beach-prep diet by moving to one that was more manageable. After mulling it over, you decided to switch to the Arctic Circle Beach diet. This diet allows 8000 more calories a day than the one you're currently starving on and the weight loss goal is very manageable because you only have to lose enough to fit into a polar bear Snuggie.

When you announced the diet you were about to start to your entire email group, old acquaintances you bump into soon after nervously ask you how the diet's going. When they hear "Successful beyond my wildest dreams", you get a kick out of their shocked expressions. Then you tell them "Ha ha, Gotcha…. Nah, I gave it all I had for as long as I could endure the grueling demands, but quit that nightmare scam once I realized it was more like a starvation diet. I won't get into the gory details, but those 24 hours I was on it were some of the darkest hours of my entire life."

You still go on a Spring diet every year, but you are years past the time when you used to worry about the goal most Spring dieters have about fitting into a sexy bathing suit. You diet now each Spring because you worry about being able to fit into your pool.

Your only diet discipline you have that you can take some pride in is at least you were able to stop snacking while you are waiting to have your midnight snack.

You can tell your chubby neighbor's Spring diet didn't work when the first time he went in his pool your basement flooded.

You've considered writing a tell-all book about 101 scam diets that actually make you gain weight.

People are always curious to know what diet you're on for the same reason they'll ask a guy with 12 kids what type of discount Dollar store condoms he uses for birth control.

You complained to your dietician that he's a complete hack because you've tried every diet he has suggested and none of them work. He politely informed you that the evidence from all the studies that have been done on the subject concluded you shouldn't expect to see any positive results unless you've dieted for more than 3 days.

Surprisingly, overweight acquaintances are always telling you they're dying to know what diet you're on now, but it's only so they can rule out the ones that definitely won't work.

You declare success on a diet the same way the government does: you decreased the rate of increase in your weight gain before you claimed victory.

Thankfully, you never have to ask your wife now how her diet's going. That's because you've figured out a way to accurately estimate if she has lost any weight yet based on how high you bounce off the mattress after she plops into bed at night.

You've added 10 pounds each year for the last 10 years to the amount you originally said you had to lose on your first Spring crash diet before you'd ever be seen in public in a bathing suit again.

Everybody in your family is so fat, the best diet you were ever on was the "show up for dinner 5 minutes late" left-over crumbs diet.

If your New Year's resolutions for the last 3 years were to lose 30 pounds, then 40 pounds, then 50 pounds.

Everyone keeps your Christmas card picture on their refrigerator when they have a New Year's resolution dieting goal. It turns out it's the best, scared straight scenario to illustrate what the worst thing is that could happen when you overindulge for the holidays.

Whenever you notice you've been served an unusual meal by your wife that you've never seen before, you've learned not to ask questions. That's because you know it's likely leftover diet food from her latest failed diet and she secretly wants to see if eating it would make you gain 10 pounds too. Thankfully, you've seen this movie before so you secretly added a daily supplement of a Double Whopper, an order of super-sized fries and a

24-ounce chocolate milk shake on your drive home from work. This defensive maneuver successfully counteracted the effects of the diet food until it was gone because you don't even want to think of the dire consequences of committing the ultimate betrayal of losing weight on her diet food.

When your wife blamed you for the communication problems in your marriage she said it was because you never listen to anything she says anymore. You disputed her groundless allegation and explained in a recent article in the New England Journal of Medicine they've found indisputable evidence that shows a strong correlation between failed wife diets and increases in selective hearing disorders. When she gave you a shocked look and asked "What did you just say to me?", you told her "Sorry to confuse you. It's not your selective hearing that gets worse, it's mine."

You despise dieting, but you do have a special place in your heart for the last day of any diet, when 99.9% of the people who've tried it quit in disgust over their disappointing results. When you've finally reached the "What difference does it make anyway? I haven't lost an ounce in 3 weeks so why don't I just get it over with and start feeding my fat face again?" moment of truth, the epic binge eating crash that follows somehow makes the suffering from dieting all worthwhile.

Your husband doesn't know that you know he's been wearing a fake hearing aid for the last 10 years. You don't mind though because he doesn't know you've been on a placebo diet for the last 20 years.

You end up using all your fad diet books as milkshake coasters so you don't completely waste your money.

It's ironic to you that you've noticed most strangers you meet always greet you with a similar expression. That's got to be because you're just not familiar with what a "It would be a great icebreaker, but boy would it be one hell of a dumbass question to ask him how the diet's going" expression looks like.

Depressed friends who have failed miserably on New Year's resolution diets always look forward to meeting up with you at an annual social gathering in late January every year. Somehow spending time with you always helps restore a little bit of their shattered confidence. Even though they had thought things couldn't get any worse, you have helped them realize they're still about a thousand Double Whoppers away from hitting rock bottom.

You're so desperate and frustrated at this point in your overweight life, you're willing to make any change necessary – and you mean any change – just so long as it doesn't involve crossing any of your red lines against eating less or exercising more.

When you're trying hard and doing well on your latest diet, your understanding wife is surprisingly supportive of you and thinks you're being a little too hard on yourself. That's why, for once in her life, without a word of protest she lets you order whatever you want at your favorite fast food drive thru, but only when you order while you're talking in your sleep.

To you, of all the terrible diets you've been on the ones where you're required to count calories are the worst. Your problem is you keep losing your count when you're counting calories on these diets because you've always enjoyed snacking on Twinkies and Cheetos when you do math problems.

You get all excited when your wife tells you after every 'All U Can Eat' type of vacation "We're both going on a diet now before we explode." From experience, you know neither of you has any willpower anymore and you'll both be quitting after no more than a week or two. You're always willing to make that sacrifice though because the pre- and post-diet pig out meals are always some of your lifetime-best epic junk food eating frenzies.

You don't get the point of all those gimmicky calorie counting diets. Even when you were very disciplined about keeping an accurate count each day, you always seemed to be done counting the daily 2000 calorie limit no later than 7:00 a.m. They never explained what you're supposed to do about the thousands of calories you consume after that, so that's why you ended up quitting after 2 weeks after gaining 30 pounds in 15 days on their "30 days lose 15 pounds" diet.

Your normal post-diet conversation with friends goes something like: "I haven't seen you in a while. Did you end up losing any weight on that diet you were on the last time we talked?" To which you reply "I knocked 50 pounds off my peak weight." When they get a strange look on their face and say "I hate to say it, but I gotta' admit it definitely doesn't look it." That's when you explain "Well duhhh… That's because I gained 49 of them back. You should have seen me a couple of weeks ago."

As you've advanced in years, you've come to realize many of the truths you thought were true in your youth have all been disproven. This can be a disconcerting shock and make you wonder if anything you think you know is actually true. That's why you're so thankful for the fat people in your life. With absolute certainty, you know you can count on every fat person you've ever known to fill you in on their latest diet plans without being asked in the first 5 minutes you talk to them. As a double boost of confidence, when you catch up with them in person you can be sure beyond the shadow of a doubt that they will never, ever look like they've lost an ounce.

Of course you could never open your mouth about it, but you secretly believe your wife is in denial about setting realistic goals whenever she's on a diet. Just when I thought things were going well on her latest one, she told me she was quitting. When I made my usual attempt to console her to find out what went wrong, she explained "Everything was going great until I read a recent article in my Woman's World magazine that said 'shrink resistant' yoga pants are to blame for a supernatural phenomenon that is causing women's butts all over America to become shrink resistant too. Once I discovered this, of course I realized there was no sense in dieting anymore given that my butt growth is due to a baffling scientific mystery. So, the next time you try to fool me with your pathetic empathy act and imply the actual problem is that somehow I lack the willpower and discipline needed to lose weight, don't say I didn't warn you about what happens to you next."

Never, ever attempt to commiserate with a wife by saying "I know you worked so hard and had such high ambitions, so I just wanted to say I'm sorry your diet didn't work out" when her diet didn't work out. If you're dumb enough to try, at least try to hide your amazement if she explains "Thanks, but you don't know what you're talking about. I consider it a fabulously successful diet and achieved 9 of my 10 goals. The only goal I didn't achieve was the weight loss, which I now know wasn't humanly possible on that diet anyway. Otherwise, it was a 90% success and you want to call that a failure?!?" Unless you're a big dummy or some type of glutton for punishment, that should be a good indicator how unwise it would be for you to ever mention the taboo word 'diet' again for the rest of your marriage.

Around late March each year, the first emotion of Spring for every overweight beachgoing American woman is stark terror about how she's ever going to fit into an itsy-bitsy, teeny weeny bikini in time for the summer beach season. Thankfully, at this moment of crisis, their unrivaled American drive and determination that has made us the envy of the free world kicks in. Like our forefathers, they gain laser focus to make the ultimate, patriotic sacrifice if necessary to achieve their weight loss goals, just so long as it doesn't involve the traitorous American behavior of eating right and exercising.

If you ever see a guy casually reading a Sports Illustrated with a fork stuck in his neck at an emergency room, I'm confident I have a good hunch how it got there. My educated guess is the last words he said to his wife were "Heh… what gives? Didn't you tell me not more than one week ago that you were going to go on a diet to lose 30 pounds? If I heard what I thought I heard, what in thee hell kind of phony tabloid diet would actually allow you to be scarfing down that two-foot-long Twix bar?" Anyway, this is my theory that I'm sure probably sounds a little far-fetched, yet that's how it happened to me.

I don't think a lot of women actually read the small print in those gimmicky tabloid diets they're always trying. If they did, they'd realize they're all scams and wouldn't even risk getting suckered. I love the one you always see in the grocery store magazine rack with a shock headline like "3 inches off your waist in 30 days!!!" From what I've observed, if by some miracle the diet actually worked, they don't tell you that you don't actually lose the 3 inches permanently. If you read the full disclosure, it turns out they just 'relocate' to a posterior area, most likely her butt, where she can't see them anymore. When this happens, the poor woman who got bamboozled only realizes she's been scammed once it's too late. She'll know she was hoodwinked when she notices she can't hear any of the great compliments people are giving her about how slim her waist is because her butt cheeks block her ears now when she sits.

10

ALL U CAN EAT UNTIL YOUR BUTT IS STUCK TO THE SEAT

THE CLOSEST COMPETITION to Sumo wrestling in the United States occurs when 2 legendary, 500+ pound, human land masses eye each other up as they're racing like a couple of brontosauruses for the last piece of lemon meringue pie at the All U Can Eat dessert bar. To think that admission is free to have a front row seat observing one of these epic human hippopotamus battles and listening to the crashing sounds of the belly bashing violence makes you wonder why any American lifetime buffet patron would ever pay to watch a ho-hum, 'genuine' Sumo wrestling match.

Your wife won't go to breakfast with you at All You Can Eat buffets anymore because you always stay so long she has to hurry home to start cooking to keep you from complaining about why dinner is late.

Regular customers can always tell when you're finally just about done eating dinner at the All U Can Eat buffet when you announce "Oh my God! What have I done? Just look at the time! I've got to get home or I'm going to be late for breakfast!"

You don't fear death because you didn't realize you were being warned when the wisest man you ever knew told you "If you keep on eating the way you do, most likely you're going to die at an All U Can Eat place one day." Instead of being scared, all you could think was "I must be the luckiest man alive then. Just imagine if it turns out to be true: I'm going to die one day while I'm busy doing what I love to do best!"

There's a look of deep "uhhh ohhh" concern humongous people get sometimes as they finish eating at their favorite All U Can Eat joint and realize their butt is stuck to their chair as the fire alarms start going off. The only other time I've seen this exact same look before was on the Python Hunters show when one of these snakes tried to make his getaway just after he swallowed a baby hippopotamus for lunch and had an "Ohh, shhhittttt" moment. I'll admit I don't know too much about snakes, but there was no doubt this python was thinking "Stupid, stupid, stupid, how many times is it going to take before I finally learn my mom's #1 lesson 'Always practice portion control, honey.'"

You have the distinction of being the only person in recorded history who's ever left one All U Can Eat joint to go eat at another one.

Your date seemed a little nervous about why you brought your pajamas and a pillow on your dinner date, so she told you there was no guarantee you'd get lucky on your first date. That's when you felt obliged to tell her "I'm so sorry. I know what it looks like, but it's not what you think. It's an All U Can Eat place we're going to and sometimes I have to wait awhile till I can squeeze out the door I came in when I overdo it a little. Nothing for you to worry about though. I've always paid for an Uber for my dates when this has happened before."

When you go to an all you can eat restaurant, you stop at the entrance now and measure how much room you have to expand before you get stuck again. You would never suffer this 'lightweight' humiliation on your free time, but your boss told you he was going to fire you the next time you were late getting back from lunch even if the fire department was willing to back your alibi.

You've been sued after one of your shirt buttons shot a waiter's eye out after a buffet bonanza sneeze.

When you started counting your steps on your Fitbit to improve your fitness, you got sick and tired of counting every step all day long so you started counting the steps for just one trip to and from the buffet line and then multiplied by 20 to get your daily total.

You're the type who could be asked with disbelief at an All U Can Eat buffet "You're not done with breakfast yet?!?" and you'll reply "What are you talking about? I finished breakfast an hour ago. It was so late though, I took a short break and then started eating an early lunch."

You haven't figured out yet why an air raid shelter alarm goes off, a red siren starts flashing and the staff mans the battle stations every time you walk into an All U Can Eat buffet.

You would think I would have had a satisfied and delightful feeling after a lifelong mystery that I'd always wondered about was finally resolved. Surprisingly, it wasn't a big deal to me at all. The weirdest thing I experienced after I realized I had finally eaten all I could eat at an All U Can Eat was that I still felt hungry afterwards.

Your wedding reception was at a Golden Corral buffet so you didn't do the Chicken Dance until 12 hours later, just before everyone was ready for dessert.

For the majority of American couples who think it would be good for the relationship to start spending more time together doing things that are fattening, the perfect solution is an All U Can Eat buffet.

When the All U Can Eat restaurant owner saw me sitting there at closing time, I'm sure he assumed I didn't want to leave because I was still in shock that I had finally figured out the eternal mystery of what 'all you can eat' means. I actually did find out what it means, but it wasn't like any of the other mind-blowing discoveries I've made in my life. When I knew I had unlocked the answer to this ancient eating mystery, I didn't leave because I had placed an order on Amazon and was waiting for my FedEx to arrive because all this revelation did was cause my 'one size fits all' overalls to explode.

You've had so many close calls from dangerously over-eating at buffet restaurants, you finally admitted how completely irresponsible you'd been by having so many near death encounters simply because you can't control what you eat. That's why you vowed that you were going to start acting like a more mature adult for the first time in your life and make some responsible changes. You refuse to live in denial anymore and now carry your Last Will & Testament with you wherever you go. Before you'll agree to lift a fork at an All U Can Eat joint now, you sign over the medical power of attorney to the buffet manager for your medical care since there's got to be at least a 99% chance you'll die in a buffet line one of these days.

As you've packed on an impressive amount of heft, you start getting into territorial fights with other hippopotamic land masses like yourself at All U Can Eat joints. Thankfully, since it was your first offense, the first time you were arrested the cop lessened the charge from an assault in the buffet line to an assault on the buffet.

It's a clear sign you have an overeating issue if you've ever had your mail temporarily delivered to an All U Can Eat restaurant while you were waiting to lose enough weight to be able to squeeze back out the door.

Friends know you're planning on a record-breaking day at the All U Can Eat buffet when you spray WD-40 on your butt, belly, elbows and love handles in the parking lot before you go in. If the restaurant staff is willing to assist, you'll have a good chance of squeezing out the door 8 hours later when you're done eating if they don't mind teaming up to do a tush push out the exit.

All the women were wondering what the fat guy was doing alone in their Lamaze class until you raised your hand to ask the instructor "All this baby delivery stuff is great, but when do you cover python breathing lessons after they swallowed more than they bargained for or am I in the wrong breathing lesson class?"

To everyone who knows you, they will consider your death premature if your heart attack occurs when you're only on your 5th serving at your favorite All U Can Eat buffet.

People think it's strange you don't like to eat alone at an All U Can eat buffet because you're not much of a conversationalist when you are laser-focused on scarfing down as much chow as you can. You've learned from prior, near-death experiences though that, when you're not watching what you eat, it's wise for you to have someone nearby to do it for you. That's why a common trait between all of your closest friends is they know the Heimlich maneuver and how to use an AED.

Your presence at the All U Can Eat buffet creates a subtle irony that none of the other patrons are aware of as yet. If you're able to get to eat all you can eat, not only won't there be enough left for any other customers to be able to find out if they can eat all they can eat, but they're probably won't even be enough left for them to get second helpings.

Your dad always told you "You can't compete like a champion on an empty stomach", back when you were on your high school cross country track team. Even though that was many years and a few hundred pounds ago, you still follow your dad's advice to this day. That's why reporters were shocked when you explained to them why you went to your favorite 'All U Can Eat' buffet for breakfast before winning your county's annual July 4th hot dog eating contest.

When you go to an All U Can Eat buffet, all the other patrons stop eating all they can eat to stare in amazement at how much you can eat.

Young philosophy students quietly observe you gorging at All U Can Eat restaurants to try to unlock the answer to the age-old mystery about what happens when a human bottomless pit meets an unlimited burger bar.

You've gotten so fat, eating out has become a risky business for you. Nowadays your survival regularly depends on at least 4 or 5 available Good Samaritans locking arms to form a chain to perform the Heimlich maneuver. When they're successful, you consider this an inconvenient, yet necessary, part of your normal All U Can Eat restaurant digestive process before you're able to visit the dessert tray.

Believe it or not, sometimes your true intention is to avoid attracting any attention and just have a quick soup and salad for lunch. When some of your frenzied, loyal fans catch sight of you though and give you a standing ovation when you walk into the restaurant, it always inspires you to set yet another personal record at the All U Can Eat wiener buffet.

You get tearjerker goodbyes from your family when they know you're going to an All U Can Eat restaurant because they understandably wonder if they'll ever see you again after they haven't heard from you in 2 days.

As you sat quietly chomping on your 10th double cheeseburger, you chuckled to yourself about the amazing revelation you just had that none of the other patrons had any idea about. After your pants split, you realized you'd actually solved the eternal philosophical mystery about what would happen if an irresistible force met an immovable object. After all this time, who would have thought this mystery would have been solved by wearing 'one size fits all' clothes to an All U Can Eat buffet? It seems so obvious to you now, but of course you should have known the pants were no match against your appetite.

You have a cheering section next to your reserved MVP seating area at your favorite All U Can Eat restaurant.

Your wife filed a missing person's report one time when they found you 3 days after you disappeared at a 24/7 All U Can Eat as you were just about to finally have some dessert.

You have no fear that your death will come as a surprise to you when it happens. Your buffet buddies have helped you understand, as all of them who spend as much time there as you understand, there's a 99% chance you'll die at an All U Can Eat buffet.

You still have sexual fantasies about an all-nighter, but now they're always about spending the night at your favorite 24/7 All U Can Eat diner.

You've had breakfast, lunch and dinner at the same All U Can Eat diner without leaving.

Nothing irritates you more than the blatant audacity of diners that advertise 'All U Can Eat!' right next to the sign that lists the daily closing times.

When you wear a bladder bag to an All U Can Eat restaurant, curious observers are always perplexed. They're puzzled about whether you don't want to interrupt your eating for bathroom breaks or you're nowhere near being done eating yet and know you probably won't fit through the bathroom door in 3 or 4 hours when you need to take your first piss.

All U Can Eat restaurant owners have stopped pulling the fire alarm to trick you into leaving like they used to. They're painfully aware now that it's no use after a certain point of no return in your epic pigout when they know you'll have to digest for at least 6 hours before you'll be able to fit back out the door.

You think one of the most courageous businesses in America is The Golden Corral. After seeing how much their best customers are able to scarf down at one sitting, to courageously keep offering All U Can Eat just to maintain our world domination in the number of hippopotamic land masses we have is what modern American patriotism is all about.

As much as it annoys you to no end, before you go back to the buffet line for your 4th serving, you know you need to check to see if you still fit out the restaurant door first so you're not late getting back to work – again - from your lunch hour.

When an old friend you hadn't seen in a while sees you again at the Golden Corral, he says "Wow, this is like déjà vu. Didn't I just see you in here last week?" so you tell him "Yehhh…I was just about to finish that meal when you walked in."

Your wife won't go to breakfast with you at All You Can Eat buffets anymore because you're always there for so long she has to rush to make dinner as soon as you get home.

On your first date with your future wife, she saw a sleeping bag and pillow in the back seat as she was about to get in your car. When she saw these, she told you "I'm not that type of girl" and started to walk back to the house. That's when you told her "Wait, I can explain everything. It's a complete misunderstanding. I just wanted to take you to my favorite All U Can Eat buffet so I could show off a little in front of my fan club, but sometimes when I overdo it I can't fit back out the door for a while. I didn't want to embarrass you by not being prepared so I only brought these just in case you wanted to take a nap while I was digesting."

After 5 or 6 hours, you can tell when the restaurant owner is getting antsy about you taking up a whole table to yourself because waiters have stopped by your table 5 times in the last 20 minutes asking if you'd like a dessert menu yet.

The 'All U Can Eat' restaurant staff stared at you with such utter disbelief when they saw you getting up to leave, you felt obliged to explain "I know what you're all thinking: 'lightweight', right? The truth is I only get 2 hours for lunch on my new job and I'm already 15 minutes late getting back to work. I promise I'll be back on my first day off to give you a performance worthy of your admiration."

You've asked to get your hand stamped at an All U Can Eat restaurant so you could get back in after you went home to change into bigger clothes.

At All U Can Eat joints, you always eat like you're waiting for a contest judge to do a 10 second count down before he declares a winner for the championship eating performance of the day.

When you're at an All U Can Eat restaurant, if the numbskull waiter asks "Can I bring you a dessert menu?", you tell him "Nice try buddy. Why don't you come back and ask me that same question again in about 3 or 4 hours?"

The owner of the All U Can Eat restaurant you regularly eat at doesn't let his nagging fear of you putting him out of business consume him. He's usually able to comfort himself that everything will be alright because he knows after 7 or 8 hours you'll usually leave, voluntarily, once you realize you can't fit through the bathroom door anymore.

Enormous people have problems non-fat people couldn't possibly understand. If you don't believe me, when was the last time you were at an All U Can Eat buffet and split your pants? Before you answer, the story gets worse. When this happened, you were still hungry, so you decided to get your hand stamped to go home and change into bigger clothes, but then discovered you couldn't squeeze out the exit door. With no viable options left, you stripped down to your underwear and just knew, from all the times it had happened before, that you wouldn't get one uninterrupted moment of peace as curious customers kept coming up to your table and asking "Are you a real Sumo wrestler?"

You made a 24/7 All U Can Eat breakfast joint change its name from 'All U Can Eat' to 'All U Can Eat Before Sundown'.

You're such a legend where you come from, whenever you go to All U Can Eat buffets now, the manager and armed security guards meet you out front and tell you "We don't want no trouble, but are you just here for lunch or do you plan to try to set another 3-day personal eating record? I do apologize that I have to ask this of one of our best customers but the regular buffet lunch is still the low low price of $12.99 for people with normal, human appetites. If you're just here to cause trouble again by trying to break your all-time personal eating record though, the new price is $1299.00 and there are no monthly payment plans available to allow you to come in here to eat all you can eat.

You're beginning to fear you may have an addiction because you're out at the bar till last call most nights, but yours is a Shoney's endless burger bar dependency.

When you go out to dinner with friends, no one ever asks you anymore "Do you have a favorite place you'd like to go to?" That's because no one wants to listen to you go on and on about your legendary past eating feats, which they've heard a thousand times before, while waiting 8 hours for you to finish at your favorite All U Can Eat.

You're the type who could be asked with disbelief at an All U Can Eat buffet "You're not done with breakfast yet?!?" and you'd reply "What are you talking about? I finished breakfast an hour ago, but it was so late I started eating my lunch early."

Even if you are the most loving and caring person alive, beware of ever coming to the aid of a helpless chubby lady at the Golden Corral when she innocently asks

"Would you mind giving me a hand to get out of my chair?" If you agree to help, a minute later you'll quickly realize you're in for more than you bargained for. As she's bent over with the chair stuck to her butt and you're lathering the top of her exposed butt cheeks with hamburger grease to loosen things up, you can hear your phone is blowing up. If you had the time to answer, you'd know your Good Samaritan video just hit 1 million views on Instagram. You'd also know the entire social media world seems to be waiting with bated breath for the posting of the even funnier video of you tumbling over backwards after you finally pull the chair off.

You advertise at local schools that you are a specialized type of emergency responder who's available 24/7 on a moment's notice to clean up after cafeteria food fights for free.

However long you live, the sweetest compliment you ever received was when the fattest, regular customers at your favorite All U Can Eat restaurant told you "You know what you are? You're nothing but a big show off. That's what you are. What are we supposed to eat now that you're here?"

After your most epic overeating performance ever, you had to wait for a FedEx overnight delivery before you could leave an All U Can Eat restaurant because it contained a change of clothes that were 3 sizes bigger than the ones you were wearing.

In the rare moment you're not eating at your favorite All U Can Eat diner, the waitress assumes you're just establishing when you're finally done with lunch so you won't be late to start eating dinner.

Your most difficult career decision ever occurred on a long business trip when you had just pulled into your favorite All U Can Eat place for lunch before an important afternoon meeting and you'd already split all your other pants.

They said it was against their policy to give doggy bags at the new All U Can Eat in your town, so, even though you'd already had enough to eat, you stayed to overeat for another 5 hours just out of spite.

The All U Can Eat owner admitted to the fire department he panicked and pulled the fire alarm when he ran out of food because he couldn't think of any other way to get you to leave before closing time.

Your exhausted waitress can finally tell you're done with your 'all you can eat' buffet breakfast when you ask her for a lunch menu.

Whenever someone like you asks strangers if they have a minute to give you a hand at an All U Can Eat restaurant, you have no idea how much your request secretly horrifies them. Their minds start racing when they wonder if you mean giving you CPR, the Heimlich maneuver or help pulling off the chair that's stuck to your butt. With you, it's usually all three of those requests at the same time. If they agree to help, they disappear as fast as they can when they're done because they aren't sticking around for the "one more small favor" you need of helping you squeeze through the bathroom door.

When you were working out at the gym, everyone called you buff. Now that you do your workouts at the Golden Corral, they call you buffet.

At this point in America's obesity crisis, you've really got to wonder what is still considered a criminal offense for indecent exposure and what's just a normal, everyday, 'nothing to see here', spontaneous wardrobe failure at an All U Can Eat buffet. I was thinking about that today while I was innocently scooping some mashed potatoes onto my plate at a buffet line when a raw boob whapped against my forearm. At first I was nervous because I had no idea if it belonged to a man or woman. Thankfully it turned out to be just another man boob, plopped where it shouldn't be, that had escaped from the Carhartt overalls of the enormous guy next to me who was bent over desperately trying to reach a slice of Coconut Cream pie. I breathed a huge sigh of relief to discover I'd only been violated by a man boob, but if this doesn't qualify as indecent exposure that should carry a mandatory minimum Federal sentencing of 10 years, then nothing does. Mark my words though, if we keep enforcing these laws like jaywalking, it's only a matter of time before these

shameless exhibitionists are going to become embold-
ened enough to start a Sumo wrestler Golden Corral
lunch group.

The Philadelphia Eagles have been incorrectly credited
as the inventor of the "Tush Push" play where they help
their quarterback score by getting pushed over the goal
line by his burly teammates. My Overeaters Anonymous
group at the Golden Corral have been running 'tush
push' plays for years now when one of us loses track of
how much he's eaten and needs to be rescued. When
someone in our group overdoes it, sometimes he'll need
some "4th and goal to go" help from his overeater line-
men to push his fat ass out the exit door so he can get
back to work on time after his lunchbreak. Now that the
NFL has stolen the trademark to our technique, they've
warned us that they'll sue the next time one of our
members is stuck in the exit door and asks for a little
tush push help, so we've had to resort to having the fire
department use the Jaws of Life now.

The entire trucking industry in America is required by law
to have placards on the back of their trailers that warn
other drivers behind them they take wide right turns.
Obviously, this 'common sense' legislation must have
been enacted when truckers were hitting cars all the
time when they turned because drivers had no idea they
needed so much extra room. If this makes perfect sense
to create safety laws like this in the trucking industry, I
ask you "Why don't they introduce bills in congress to
protect the rights of daily victims of accidents from all

the 18-wheeler sized regulars at All U Can Eat joints? I've never been a political activist and am actually a little shocked how passionate I've become about this singular issue. Like our forefathers, if you had just been face-planted into a tray of mashed potatoes for the third time in one week by one of the butt cheeks of a tubbo who turned abruptly without signaling, you'd be fightin' mad too. You can see how easy it is now to start a war when you go around blatantly disrespecting people's human rights. That's why, if every 400 pounder would voluntarily wear a flashing yellow CAUTION sign at buffets to warn innocent bystanders about an upcoming wide right turn, I think there's an outside chance we could still avoid a second Civil War.

When you get up to go to the dessert bar at an All U Can Eat joint, your wife grabs your wrist and tells you "Stop right where you are. I'm going to need to do some measurements first." At that point you become fidgety and anxious waiting for your seamstress's critical circum-ference result. If it has increased any more than 6 inches since you arrived, you know your dessert options will be limited to healthy fruit bowls instead of the salad bowl of ice cream with hot fudge chocolate sauce you were crav-ing. It's all about her after all and she doesn't have the patience any more to have a leisurely after dinner chat like you used to while waiting 8 hours for you to digest enough to squeeze back out the exit door.

11

VICTORIA'S BARELY KEPT SECRETS

IT MIGHT BE time to start thinking about going on a diet when yoga pants look so ridiculous on you now, the only way you can salvage any trace of self-respect is to start wearing your Sumo wrestling diaper over them when you go shopping at Walmart.

When hip hugger jeans first came out, women loved the new seductive look and men went crazy about being able to sneak a peek at a sexy butt crack. America has evolved since those days long ago and now the design has been updated to adapt to the needs of our rapidly expanding figures. They still sell the original, antique jeans that display the one butt crack, but that type now seems destined for the Smithsonian. The wildly popular 3 butt crack hip hugger jeans are all the rage these days and are flying off the shelf for the typical, 'objects in the mirror appear smaller than actual size' butts on 90% of American women.

You've gotten stuck halfway in a clothes donation box like Pooh Bear trying to retrieve one of your bags of "As God is my witness, I'll never wear these fat clothes again!" clothes after a successful diet celebration pigout that got a little out of hand.

You add about $5000 a year in new clothes to the 'clothes that don't fit' section of your closet.

As you've gained a ton of weight, to keep your pants up you have regressed from a belt to suspenders to suspension bridge cables.

As a 40-something year old guy, there's no denying anymore that you're getting in worse shape when you have to move from a training bro to a sedentary push up bra.

People think you're trying to be stylish by having writing on the butt of your pants, but when you buy your astronomical size the DOT regulations actually require a 'Wide Load' warning in neon colors.

You never bother asking questions at department stores anymore because all those store clerks in the men's department are born wise asses. When I told one recently that I looked through everything and couldn't find anything in my size he told me "Listen pal, no offense, but just think how dumb that sounds to me. Like duhhhh… How could we carry something in your size when you keep inventing 'never before seen' sizes every couple of weeks? See what I'm saying?"

No one ever tells you "Ooohhh, I love your dress. It looks so good on you. Where did you get it?!?" like women who are in great shape often hear. It's not like you don't get new dress compliments of your own, but you would prefer not to share any of the praise you get from acquaintances when it's more like "I just love, love, love your new dress. I've been looking for a tent exactly like it that sleeps 8 for our next family camping trip. Do you know if it's waterproof?"

You love your wife's new skin tight, hip hugger jeans because her ass cleavage makes a great beer koozie now when you're sitting on the couch together watching TV.

When your wife tells you she can't fit into any of her old jeans, that might not sound surprising until you find out that when a wife uses the word 'old' to describe clothes she means anything she bought more than 3 weeks ago.

The problem with a lot of American women is once none of the sexy clothes at Victoria's Secrets fit them anymore, instead of being practical and shopping for Fruit of the Loom lingerie at Walmart, it looks like they started shopping at Victoria's Barely Kept Secrets.

The only unique thing about you is that the fashion industry hasn't come up with a size to describe you yet.

You can never tell anyone your clothes sizes for presents because all yours say "One size fits all".

You don't like wearing "One size fits all" clothes because they're always a little tight in the waist and butt.

The best thing about shopping at the chain of Big and Fat stores is even when the line is out the door it turns out there are only 6 or 7 guys in front of you.

You have no idea why they would call your new outfit a wraparound dress when it looks like a hospital gown on you.

You've always preferred 'push up' bras but the only one that fits you now is a 'Pull 'em up, pack 'em in, then push 'em up' bra.

After you bought your first pair of hip hugger jeans, you took them back to the store to return them thinking they were defective because yours created an optical illusion in your mirror by showing 3 butt cracks.

It's a slippery slope you negotiate when you decide to give clothes to a wife as birthday presents. If you're ever dumb enough to do it, you won't believe the price you'll pay for buying new jeans that actually fit perfectly, when you can't stop stuttering as you try to explain how you knew they should be 3 sizes bigger than last year's.

You've returned 'one size fits all' clothes because they didn't fit.

People can tell when you must have really loved what was served for dinner whenever you had to change into bigger clothes at least twice before you finished eating.

You don't realize how ridiculous you sound trying to salvage some self-respect when you tell people who've asked "This outfit? No, it's not one of those 'one size fits all' male Snuggies. Don't be ridiculous. I may not look it, but I'm way too small to be wearing one of those ridiculous outfits. This is only a XXXXXXL."

Your wife has sewn sweaters for the whole family from your bellybutton lint.

Even though you have a strong suspicion it had, you couldn't tell for sure if your waist size had increased again. That was because when you went to try on any of your old pants to see if they would be too tight in the waist, you couldn't even pull them up past your knees to find out.

The fashion industry doesn't bother trying to come up with a size to describe someone like you anymore. It's only because when they think they've finally come up with one and are excited to have you try it on, you'll be asking "Can you show me something in the next size up? This is a little tight in the waist."

When you sort your fat clothes now after you do the laundry it's into fat, fatter and fattest piles now.

Whenever you wear a shirt to work that doesn't have ketchup and chocolate stains on it everyone says "Heh, I just love your shirt. It must be new, huh?"

You're 40 now, but for the last 32 years your mom has been buying you clothes for presents that are 2 sizes too big because she tells you "Don't worry honey, I'm sure you'll grow into them". You were doubtful at first but, you'll be darned, after all these years mom is still always right.

When you wear hip huggers, they seem to be at a complete loss as to what to try to frantically hug next to limit 'butt cheek creep' escapes.

You're proud to say that you can still wear all of your old high school dress shirts 20 years after you graduated. The one minor problem now though is you can't even come close to covering your bellybutton in any of them.

They look so ridiculous on you now, the only time you'll wear them anymore in public is at a wedding or funeral on your side of the family. At least you know when you're surrounded by family that you won't be judged unfairly since none of the other guys have been able to tuck their shirt in their pants since high school either.

You're always especially observant now about what your wife is wearing after she surprised you one time by sticking out her butt at you and asking how you thought it looked in her first pair of yoga pants. Caught completely unaware, you took a quick look and had a horrifying flashback to your army days when you jumped on the floor behind the bed and screamed "TAKE COVER!!! I think it's about to explode!!!" Whatever the response was she had hoped for, I could tell by the projectiles I began ducking that this definitely wasn't the reaction she was expecting.

As much as it bruised your ego, you felt you had no choice but to start shopping at Victor's Secrets for some confidential, middle-aged man boob and girdle lingerie to avoid being the laughingstock of your bowling league.

Any husband who has any intent of surviving in a marriage must realize he needs to carefully comb over every word he's about to say whenever he has a comment that even remotely concerns his wife's weight or shape.

When you absentmindedly told your wife "Honey, I don't think your new dress is out of style or unpopular just because you've never seen any other woman wearing one. It's probably just because they ran out of material after they made your size and had to restock first." As you heard your big, fat, stupid mouth saying this, you sensed your time on earth might be limited. It turned out to be even worse, like one of those times in life when you'd be better off deciding to learn how to juggle flaming hatchets on a unicycle while blindfolded than have to reply to her follow up question of "Just what the F... is that supposed to mean peckerhead?"

If you have a raincoat that fits, it could probably be used to keep Rhode Island from getting wet when it's raining.

The only skirt size that fits you now is an outskirt.

When your wife asked "How does my butt look in these new pants?" you were dumb enough to say "Wait a sec'. Let me run across the street so I can take it all in at once."

You've gotten so fat, the only thing in your closet that fits anymore that you wouldn't be embarrassed to be seen wearing in public are your Sumo wrestling diapers.

You had no idea when you bought the hip hugger style of pants that you'd be faced with a public indecency decision concerning what part of your hips the pants are going to hug and which part gets to moon people.

No matter what stylish new bra you buy now, the sex appeal of your cleavage is always ruined by having a bellybutton in it somewhere.

Yoga pants product engineers secretly follow you around in grocery stores to evaluate maximum elasticity testing while you're bent over checking Twinkie prices on the bottom shelf.

You don't have to wonder if your ass grew a lot over the winter when friends comment they just love your new Spring capris when they're actually the winter pants you bought 3 months ago.

The world's leading product engineers look at your yoga pants clad butt and are insanely jealous when they realize you, a lowly McDonalds cashier, solved the eternal mystery that had always escaped them on how you can get 10 pounds of crap into a 5-pound bag.

You never care too much about what's for dinner but do always check how much food there is for dinner beforehand so you can either go change into bigger clothes if it looks like a feast or have pizzas delivered if it does not.

When the pants style changed to hip huggers, the manufacturer would only sell 'hugs only some of the hips' pants for your size to avoid a big lawsuit for false advertising.

Your husband wears baggy pants all the time that look completely ridiculous on him. He only wears them because he's scared to death to tell you the truth when it would likely put you into a bloodthirsty, murderous rage. He knows he doesn't ever want to know what you would do next in your state of temporary insanity if you ever confessed to her " It's so embarrassing to admit, but none of my pants fit anymore. I've lost so much weight I need a smaller size."

When you wear a girdle it allows you to be able to comfortably rest your chin in your belly button.

When family ask what size you are for clothes presents, they know enough to add an extra size per week before your birthday.

The clothes industry doesn't bother making a size for people like you anymore. It's because even if it fit at the store changing room, they know it probably wouldn't fit once you got home after you stopped off at the Burger King drive thru on your way there because you were so hungry from trying on clothes.

When you walk in a tight dress, the movement of your butt reminds people of 4 puppies playing under a bed sheet.

You've returned shrink resistant yoga pants for what you thought was false advertising only to discover it was your shrink resistant butt that was the problem all along.

When a guy is on a date with a wife who has a humongous butt and she is advertising it in ridiculously skin-tight jeans that are causing everyone to glance at this circus-type spectacle, he's faced with a real dilemma. Everyone they pass gives him a stunned look that says "How in the world can you be acting so calm when your wife is creating such a public nuisance?". In response, he'll return an awkward expression that signals he understands their obvious concerns, yet still supports his wife's right to choose what she wears. Only married men who've been in this predicament know exactly what this look means: "I know it was selfish of me, but I was really hungry when I answered after she asked how her butt looked in those pants before we went out to dinner. I just couldn't find the words to tell her the truth without ruining 20 years of being happily married so, as much as it's uncomfortable for you, mind your own business. We're in this thing together now."

Boy would I like to get my hands around the neck of the guy who originally came up with the slang word 'phat'. The huge problem this created for us married guys is its homonym 'fat', which is most often used in an American marriage to describe 75% or more of a wife's clothes. I have never stayed on top of the created words from Gen X/Y/Z that you won't find anywhere in Webster's unabridged dictionary, but my wife always has. That's how I became impossibly stupid enough to think what she used to call her 'fat' clothes, which live a lonely life in a darkened section of the closet, were actually cool 'phat' clothes now. Of course, a misconception like this would result in a ticking time bomb. Innocently enough, disaster finally struck when she came out of a dressing room one day and asked me if the new 'hip hugger' jeans design made her butt look fat. I of course assumed she meant 'phat' and told her the most glowing praise my puny man brain could come up with on short notice "Honey….I can't lie: no pants have ever made your butt look phatter." That was 10 years ago and yet not a day goes by that I don't get some type of threatening reminder to never, ever comment on her appearance again with any word invented after my Baby Boom generation.

One day, early on in our marriage, my wife pulled down all the shades and then showed me 5 bulging, heavy, industrial-strength Hefty trash bags in the cellar. I was puzzled what all the secrecy was about, so she told me "Your wife needs a favor from you. I need you to get rid of this evidence, if you know what I'm saying. Don't look inside any of them, but I want you to drag them out to your car, put them in your trunk and drive a long way away from here after midnight. When I used to have this job, I would dump them in a swamp next to a deserted highway somewhere where no one would ever find them. Now that we're family, I want you to be involved in the family business. You need to promise me too that you'll never mention this to anyone or ever ask any questions about this. If, in some unlikely circumstance someone was to ask you about this, you don't know nuttin' about it, capisce?" When she finished, I was completely horrified and said "Oh my God! I had no idea you work for the mob!!!" After she apologized for all the confusing drama and explained what was in the bags, we came to a compromise. She agreed it would be a better idea to donate all the 'bikini body' clothes she bought after her successful diet 6 months ago, which don't fit anymore now, to Goodwill. In return, I agreed to find a donation site at least 500 miles away from our house and never breathe a word of this to anyone if I didn't want to get whacked.

Lululemon's greatest fear is that their engineering lab maximum elasticity tests on yoga pants might one day prove to be inadequate due to the exponential expansion of modern American women's butts. After all, the popularity of the pants comes from their designed, skin-tight sex appeal. Consequently, it would be ridiculous for them to make a baggy 6XL size that is needed for upwards of 90% of female Walmart shoppers. Without a larger size available, the impending nightmare they most fear is women with humongous butts will feel forced to stuff more and more ass into size Medium pants until they surpass the previously assumed infinite limits of stretchability. At this tipping point, all it would take to create a catastrophic disaster at Walmarts throughout the land is a seemingly harmless stocking change. On a day when there's an inexplicable, nationwide mandate to move the Twinkies from the 3rd shelf to the bottom shelf in the snack aisle, it's likely that yoga pants would start exploding all over the country until the Twinkies were pulled from the shelf. Of course it would be too late for Lululemon. All of the investigations, lawsuits, punitive damages and bankruptcy would follow shortly afterwards and the only place you'd ever see yoga pants again would be between the hula hoop and the Easy bake oven at the Smithsonian.

Finally, there's some merit to a lawsuit against Victoria's Secrets for a long-awaited charge of discrimination against chubby, middle-class white men. In today's whacky America, Victoria's Secrets knows they're on a slippery slope by refusing to offer any 'male only' products in their stores. They did make a lame attempt to offer us some products for on-line purchase, but we're not going to be shamed anymore into shopping on-line while hiding in a closet because they somehow think we're embarrassed about how we look. Have you been to the beach lately? My guess is upwards of 90% of all middle-aged white men over 40 are at least at the training bra stage and most are closer to a DD cup. Victoria's Secret is terrified of stocking man boob bras in their stores though because they fear the exclusive, in-store experience for their women shoppers might get ruined forever. I respectfully disagree with this theory. No regular Victoria's Secret customer has ever paid any attention to fat, balding middle-aged white dudes. Why would they start noticing us once we start showing up with our beer coolers for a guy's night out trying on man boob bras? Besides, the only possible drawback I foresee is when we were in high school and couldn't get a hot girl's attention, we resorted to the locker room prank of snapping their bra straps. I can envision the possibility of some prudish, middle-aged shoppers filing complaints if they're not familiar with this mating technique. These same women would probably be insanely jealous too of the reverse discrimination freedom we're allowed of being able to flash our man boobs when they would get arrested if they did it. Other than that, I'm sure we'd learn to live with the destruction of yet another American institution, just as we do with all the other ones.

I don't claim to be an expert, but I'm pretty sure I know what's causing the troubling rate of divorce in America for most guys. Surprisingly, it concerns the wife adding a new vow on top of the ones you both originally agreed to at your wedding. Unlike the outdated love, honor and cherish vows, all wives who've experienced the life-changing ordeal of dieting for more than 2 weeks for the first time are deadly serious about their vow to never wear their 'fat' clothes again. Having learned from previous 'break the bank' experiences, all guys nervously wait to hear how much all of this is going to cost to avoid bringing everlasting shame on the family by wearing 'fat' clothes on her new bikini body. Although it was shocking, I was pleasantly pleased that the amount was nowhere near some of the other astronomical, unexpected costs of having a wife. It's been 20 years since that first diet though. During that time, my educated guess is we've been through the diet cycle at least 10

times. Call me stupid, but I learned even women without a trace of self-discipline always live up to their vow
of never wearing their 'fat' clothes again. The reason for
this consistency though is, after the epic binge eating
phase following the diet crash, they can't even fit into
their old 'fat' clothes anymore, so they have no choice
other than to buy 'fatter' clothes.

Whenever your wife is pissed off about a significant
recent weight gain, for your safety, I recommend tiptoe-
ing past the closet and then running for cover if you
ever hear her cursing in there in a terrifying, profanity-
laced, demonic chant. This is always a 'strain on the
relationship' period, but there's really nothing a mere
man can do to help in a situation like this. Take my word
for it that it never gets worse than when she's furiously
moving clothes from the "As God is my witness, I'll never
wear these again!" Fat Clothes section onto the 'Active
Wear' hangars and those clothes into the "Fat Chance –
couldn't fit a leg into any of these" section. Before you
even think of it, forget about calling an exorcist. I've
called them all and they'll all tell you this is proof God is
a guy because this is a demonic possession only a successful diet can cure.

I make a good salary, but, after 30 years of marriage
we're still living paycheck to paycheck. Strangely
enough, it's all because of one stupid thing we could
never figure out how to budget when our costs got out
of control. When I think back on the causes for this, I
get this sense of deep regret that if my wife had just

followed her own advice that she always gave our boys of "I know these pants are 2 sizes too big, but – trust me – I'm sure you'll grow into them", I would be a millionaire by now. The worst thing about it is I only have myself to blame because I never had the balls to bring it up as a 'can't miss' savings idea. I think that's because I took it as a deadly warning whenever I had this idea on the tip of my tongue when my wife would stop me and say "You know, there are some great ideas that are better left unsaid – if you know what's good for you. I think this is one of them."

When you're trying on clothes in a department store and can't find anything that fits, don't ever ask a teen-age clerk for help if he looks like a born wise-ass. Some of these guys will stay in their crappy jobs for years just waiting for the moment someone like you finally com-plains "I can't seem to find anything that fits me in this crappy store. Don't you stock anything for someone my size?" At this miracle moment for him, you'll only have yourself to blame when he tells you "I'm sorry sir. I could check with my manager, but I'm pretty sure we don't have anything in your size because up till now no one has ever been your size before." and then turns in his badge and walks out of the store with his hands raised in victory.

12

———————————————

DON'T EVER LET YOUR CAREER STAND IN THE WAY OF YOUR EATING DREAMS

YOU WERE EMBARRASSED that you were required to go through retraining after your first week as a Papa John's pizza delivery driver. Even though you told your boss you were absolutely sure you were on time and delivered the correct number of boxes to every customer he told you "We're not disputing that. Even though it sounds a little unreasonable to maintain our 100% customer satisfaction rate, we've learned it really matters to our most loyal customers if the pizzas are still in the boxes when you deliver them."

You started to wonder why, on your interview with the Domino's pizza delivery manager, he asked you "We don't discriminate against hiring anyone, but don't you think there might be at least a teeny little bit of a conflict of interest for someone of your, let's say, 'hefty' size on a job like this?" All you could think to respond was "I don't want to sound like I'm one of those 'whiny complainer' types, but do you realize you've already asked me that question 5 times?"

Even though you don't get 20% tips like all the other pizza delivery drivers do, you aren't mad about it at all because you figure you only deliver about 60% of the food anyway.

When you're late for work because you overslept, you tell your boss it was because you had to finish eating in your dream. Normally he doesn't buy anyone's lame excuses for being late, but surprisingly he accepted that as a perfectly understandable excuse for a guy like you.

You got desperate at work one time and squirted a line of catsup down a frightened co-worker's forearm just before the vending machine guy all of a sudden miraculously appeared to refill the snack machines.

You get a kick out of co-workers who take the elevator down from your 12th floor office, but always take the stairs back up after lunch. Other office workers who use the elevator assume they're just getting some exercise in. The real reason is, even though the elevator says it has a 2000-pound weight capacity, they know from experience that when they're in it with you it will only go down.

The only compliment you've had lately at work was when you and your boss were stuck in an elevator. As he was gasping for air, he told you "I guess (gasp)... I was wrong about you all along....If somehow we get out of this alive (gasp,gasp) ... I hope you can find it in your heart to forgive me one day (gasp,gasp, gasp)... ...I guess I just always wrongly assumed that all oxygen thieves had to be stupid too." Then he passed out until the maintenance guy got the door open.

You'd like to pack a lunch more often for work, but you're sick and tired of co-workers excitedly whispering if anyone knows about a surprise office party when they see how full the breakroom refrigerator is.

When you tell your manager "Sorry boss, my plate is full", he assigns you the work anyway because he knows a plate isn't going to stay full around you for very long.

You call the Sears storage container on your roof rack your work lunch box.

When you ask new employees out to lunch on their first day on the job, they usually tell you "I'd love to, but for purposes of full disclosure, I don't know how to do the Heimlich maneuver and don't think I could handle doing it myself for you if I did...... in the unlikely event that was why you were inviting me".

You filed harassment charges against your boss because every time you ask if he'd approve an Amazon order for the office, he asks "I'll gladly approve, but before I do, would you like to supersize your order?"

As an office worker, you've redefined what an ass kisser is now that you can kiss your own ass instead of your boss's.

When there was a huge fire at your office building, you hurriedly evacuated with all the other employees as your building was engulfed in flames. Shortly afterwards, co-workers were in tears as they watched you strut fearlessly back into the building because they thought you'd never make it out alive. They felt such love and admiration for you when they assumed you must have been selflessly risking your life by fearlessly going back in to save someone who couldn't make it out. They were less impressed a minute later when you waddled back out, choking and gasping for air, while clutching the box of Twinkies you'd left on your desk.

When you're still at your desk after 5:00 p.m., everyone just assumes you have a toilet seat stuck to your butt again and are just waiting for everyone else to leave so you can put your trench coat on and sneak out the back way.

Co-workers understandably believe you're moonlighting as a pizza delivery driver when they see a stack of 8 pizza boxes on the front seat of your car, when the truth is you just decided to pack a lunch for work.

All U Can Eat restaurant managers always stop by your table to do some polite chatting with you, presumably to find out what you think of the food since you seem to have had at least 3 servings of everything. What they're really up to though on their charm campaign is to slyly find out where you work so they can call your boss and beg him to shorten your lunch break.

Whenever you get a new job, the first thing every company does for employee orientation is show you where the vending machines are located.

It doesn't matter where you interview, whenever a new company is interested in hiring you, they take you on a tour to show you the wide variety of vending machines, 24/7 cafeteria buffet and free break room pastries and donuts. That's when you know you have them just where you want them. After you play hard to get, they close the deal by bending their lunch break rule for you from 30 minutes to 3 hours.

When you interview for new jobs the only question you ask that will determine whether it's going to be a deal-breaker or not is always "How long is lunch break?"

When they made a strict office rule at work that you could no longer eat at your desk, you put in a ticket to have the maintenance department remove your desk.

When you've been mysteriously missing at work for a while and co-workers are starting to become worried, the first place they always look for you is the breakroom to see if you might have gotten an arm stuck again in one of the snack machines again.

You were so relieved when your company finally relaxed their clothing policy and moved to business casual. People were beginning to suspect you were just 'making it look like an accident' every time you injured a co-worker in the last 2 months after you sneezed and almost shot an eye out with a projectile button from your suit jacket.

When you got a job as a pizza delivery driver, Domino's had to start making pathetic excuses when they apologized to their best customers by explaining "For some strange reason, there's been a big demand for 'half of a pizza' delivery drivers lately and we must have mixed up your whole pizza order with one of these. You have our 100% guarantee this will never happen again."

You think it showed complete commitment to your job that you'll do whatever it takes to show up to work on time when you showed up one time with a toilet seat from a porta potty stuck to your butt.

When you tell your employees "I just had a meeting with the boss and he said we're going to have to do a little belt tightening around here", they instantly reply in unison "You're going to have to show us what you think that means."

You're always starving and feeling feint late in the after-noon at work. You're sure it's because you can never get enough to eat during your 30 minute lunch break so you've devised a plan to fix the problem by researching how pythons are able to swallow everything at once.

You took a job as a waiter one time, but quickly quit to become a busboy, even though it paid a lot less. It seemed like a bad career management move, but you did it because on that job no one cared what you ate off the customer's plate after the person who ordered it had left.

You think your resume shouts 'WINNER' because you listed you're a 6-time National hot dog eating contest champion.

You were about to be written up by human resources for violating the dress policy against wearing a mini skirt to work, but then avoided being disciplined at the last second. It was an epic 'in your face' moment to the pissed off HR lady when you grabbed the rest of your ankle length skirt out of your ass and announced 'Surprise!... Sorry for the big misunderstanding. It tends to bunch up a little between my butt cheeks as the day goes on."

When you have a meeting that goes past lunchtime, co-workers give each other 'knowing winks' and start talking about their favorite foods so they can take bets on who can get you to start drooling first.

You've never had a problem with the concept of busting your butt to achieve your personal goals. Your problem as a 'chair warmer' office worker though is every time you've ever worked your ass off before it's always made it grow – a lot.

Everyone seems to take advantage of fat people because they're the only unprotected class left in America that you can still discriminate against and get away with it. That's why you like to give advanced warnings to hecklers now by telling them, "Don't allow yourself to think just because I'm good natured about all your endless fat jokes that I'm always this easy going. Just try, even once, wrestling the last doughnut in the Dunkin' Donuts box in the breakroom away from me. I'll show you who's jolly as I belly butt your sorry ass back where you belong."

You bring a lunchbox to work but have started putting breakfast foods in it lately since, once you start munching on it, it never seems to last more than 15 minutes after you get to work.

When your new boss told you that you have half an hour for lunch break, you told him you'd have to give your notice if he couldn't give you a longer break. He was baffled about why you would need more time to eat, so you told him you agreed that was plenty of time to eat. "What's the problem then?" he asked, so you told him "Take a good look at me. 30 minutes is enough time to eat for anyone, but I need an extra hour or so to overeat."

When you pick up a drive thru order on your work lunch break, you know you have to practice extreme self-control not to eat it until you get back to work, even though you know it will be ice cold by then. It's not like you couldn't easily eat it all in the Burger King parking lot on your half hour lunch break and make it back with plenty of time to spare. The problem is, as you're painfully aware, there's a 50:50 chance you'd still be late getting back to work because you never can predict when you'll have to digest for a while until you can get the steering wheel to budge again.

When you pack a lunch for work it always becomes a late 2nd breakfast instead.

Co-workers like to be in meetings with you that go past lunchtime to see if you get desperate enough to put a foot in your mouth.

When you're forced to take the stairs to your 2nd floor office when the elevator isn't working, you call ahead and ask the company nurse to have an IV, oxygen mask and the defibrillator plungers ready just in case.

When you first started working as an undercover cop, you were a lean, mean, crime fighting machine. 10,000 Dunkin Donuts later, the boss told you he's putting you on desk duty because you only qualify as a 'fart under the covers' cop now.

Co-workers intentionally raise their voices to tell people on the phone "my plate is full" and then take bets on how long it will take you to show up sniffing around their cubicle with a fork and knife.

When people ask what type of employee you are, loyal co-workers will tell them "He's one of those passionately devoted types who will always go the extra mile... but that's only when he can't find an open fast-food drive thru."

When you're in a meeting and you announce that you would like to share a new idea, the boss stifles a giggle and says "Wonderful news. Why don't you take a minute now to 'expand' on that?" It always pisses you off that by the time everyone stops their childish backslapping and hysterical laughter afterwards, you've gotten so hungry you can never remember what your idea was anymore.

You've developed a habit of going early to all job interviews so you can check out the weight capacity of their elevator. From experience, you know you can love everything about the job, but having to walk upstairs now is a non-negotiable deal breaker at this point in your career.

When you started packing a lunch for work and leaving it on your desk, it got so distracting you couldn't get any work done. Thankfully, you were able to resolve that problem by turning it in to corporate security and giving them permission to use deadly force if you tried to get it out of their gun locker before your noon lunch break.

There was a hushed silence as you unexpectedly got up from your chair at your favorite 'All U can eat' restaurant. The staff stared at you with such disbelief as you were about to leave, you felt obligated to explain "If you think that's all I can eat, nothing could be further from the truth. I'm leaving because I could only negotiate 2 hours for lunch breaks on my new job".

None of your co-workers was surprised when you bit off your arm to avoid starvation that time you got it stuck in the snack machine and had given up when no one came to rescue you after 30 minutes.

When a big fella like you walks out of a pizza joint with a big stack of pizzas, all who witness this think only one of two things could be happening: you're either picking up your lunch or you're soon to be a former pizza delivery driver who's about to eat someone else's lunch.

When you walk up the stairs at work after lunch you amaze your co-workers, but it's only because, for a guy, you look a lot more like a pregnant woman whose contractions are less than a minute apart.

Your co-workers demonstrated how much they care for you when their puzzled Lamaze class instructor asked them why they signed up for the class to help their male boss. They explained that the elevator was broken at your office building, so you are forced to use the stairs now to get back to your 2nd floor office after your marathon 'All U Can Eat' lunches. When you reach the top step, your face is beet red and you're panting and heaving like you're in labor. At that moment, they just wanted to be able to help coach your panicked breathing until your stomach cramps are 2 minutes apart and you're ready to close down the men's room when you're ready to push.

When a nervous, new hire clerk gives you a terrified stare on his first trip on the elevator, you try to ease his fears by saying "I know what you're worried about pal. I wasn't giving you a curious look because I was considering eating you first if we ever got stuck for more than an hour. I was just noticing you look a lot like one of my old high school friends. Besides, heaven forbid it ever came to that, I already made my choice to eat the guy next to you before you even came in." This fake attempt to provide comfort to a rookie was convincing enough that he decided to start taking the stairs to your 45th floor office every day with all the other new hires who'd had an elevator trip with you.

13

HAVE SOME MANNERS!!! PLEASE DON'T EAT OUT OF THE TRASH UNTIL ALL OUR DINNER GUESTS HAVE LEFT

WHENEVER YOU'RE VISITING someone's home for the first time and, after their initial shock, the host nervously attempts a show of hospitality by saying "Uhhh… why don't you make yourself at home", you ask "Are you sure about that? Let's not waste any more time with small talk then and show me the way to the refrigerator and snack closet."

As a dinner guest, you know the host isn't bluffing that the food is all gone when the exasperated wife says "You must think I'm a terrible host. I'm deeply embarrassed to admit this, but I mistakenly thought 12 pounds of meat would have been enough for the 4 of us. If you want more to eat, it's going to be a little while because I'm going to have to sacrifice one of the kids' pets."

When people give you gifts, they always say "I can always take it back if you don't like it, but why don't you at least taste it first."

When you're a guest, you have a 6th sense about when it would be polite to stop eating after a series of questions from the host. You're pressing your luck when you answer "Yes, of course" each time you're asked "Would you like a 2nd … 3rd… 4th… 5th… helping?" You're starting to play with fire when she tells you "It's midnight, I'm exhausted and the kids have school in the morning. Don't you think you've had enough to eat by now?". You'll know you've completely worn out your welcome forever if you force her hand to tell you "Uncle. You win; I give up. You've cleaned us out better than the Grinch did in Whoville. There's nothing left to offer you but one of the children's pets. I would hate to get a reputation as a bad host so would you prefer hamster or guinea pig for your 6th and last serving I ever serve you, as God is my witness?"

To all your friends and family, you're like the anti-Grubhub delivery guy. You have the addresses of everyone you know in your phone and always call when you're in their area to let them know you're thinking of stopping in for a bite to eat. When you get there, everyone knows you so well they meet you at the front door and hand you a big bag of junk food to keep you from coming in the house and you tip them for the service and then go eat in the car.

When acquaintances have a friend like you, they've all learned the same lesson that they would never share with you which is: you won't watch what you eat so they better do it for you if they know what's good for them. They all share this same belief because they thought it was bad enough how long you stayed for dinner, but it was even worse how long it took you to digest enough to be able to squeeze back out the door.

At your current record-breaking weight, it's no surprise to anyone that you're not much of a conversationalist as a dinner guest once the meal has been served. When everyone is finished eating though, you're like a little chatterbox asking everyone "Are you gonna' eat that?... Would you mind if I licked your plate?... Can everyone please pass the leftovers to this end of the table?... This is the last time I'm going to ask you before I go search-ing for myself: are you absolutely sure there's nothing left to eat?"

When you get invited to a neighborhood cookout, all the other guests end up feeling more like they're hungry spectators at a one-man hot dog eating contest.

It's so embarrassing it's almost as if it could make you want to do the most hateful thing you could ever imag-ine, which is to eat right and exercise, to avoid the humiliation you endure whenever you're invited to social events. Even though you're clearly being discriminated against, instead of just responding, you're the only invited guest who's required to send measurements of your current circumference on your RSVP to see if you'll be eating indoors or outdoors.

People don't like to invite you to Thanksgiving because you eat so much it's going to take a miracle to squeeze you back out the door before Christmas.

It's sad, yet understandable that whenever you get invites to cookouts from the friends who know you best, yours is always an hour later than everyone else's invitation. There's no insult intended though. The people who know you best just know they've got to give their other guests a good head start before all the food miraculously disappears 20 minutes after you arrive.

A lot of neighbors put on a ridiculous display of apologies and expressions of how awful and stupid they feel for listing the wrong start time on your invitation for a summer cookout. You know the pattern well enough now though and know what they're up to and don't buy a word of their apology. I mean who gets invited to a cookout that starts at 11:00 p.m.? Unfortunately, you know you're always invited late to cookouts now so that everyone else will have a chance to eat before your onslaught on the buffet table. As an added bonus, the host knows they won't have to worry about cleaning up any leftovers and all the plates, bowls and serving spoons will have been licked clean and just need to be put into the dishwasher.

When you visit old friends, you're keenly aware that even best friends get irritated when guests wear out their welcome. That's why, even though you believe you're risking starvation, you watch what you eat so you'll be sure to be able to fit back out the door after dinner. It's a race after that of hope against hope that you can avoid passing out from hunger before you reach the nearest drive thru after you leave.

You've learned from bad experiences to load up on your 2nd serving when you're a dinner guest because even the most courteous hosts won't even ask if you want a 3rd helping, never mind 4th's, 5th's and 6th's like you get at home.

If you had been an apostle, Jesus would have misunderstood when you started sobbing hysterically when he announced that this was the Last Supper, shortly before you started to eat. The gospels might have been written differently if Jesus had to stop what he was doing and tell you "For crying out loud Harvey, stop whimpering and pull yourself together. It's my Last Supper, not yours."

No dinner host who knows you well has ever used that cheesy line on you "Are you sure you've had enough to eat? I wouldn't want to see you leaving hungry." They know they would live to regret it if they fed you more and then you had to stay another couple of hours after the other dinner guests failed on their first 3 attempts to try to 'tush push' you out of the front door.

If you'd been at the Last Supper, all of Christianity would be different today. Jesus would have been shocked when he realized there wasn't any bread left because you'd eaten every last crumb. As a result, the gospels would have been written differently when Jesus had to revise his prepared speech and say "Take one of these after-dinner thin mints and eat it in memory of me."

When you're a dinner guest, the host dreads trying to be courteous by asking the risky question "Are you sure you've had enough to eat? I wouldn't want you to tell anyone that you left hungry." As she's asking, she is careful not to divulge that there's less food in the house than when the Grinch left Cindy Lou Who's house in Whoville. If you call her bluff, you love how you force her to admit "You got me. I guess you must have already known there's nothing left when I had you lick the pot for your 6th serving. I guess we could order pizza or run to get a bag of burgers at McDonalds if you don't mind waiting? I hate to be a bad host."

Before you open your presents at your birthday party, your wife has you put on oven mitts in case any of the gifts were just microwaved.

When dinner hosts nervously ask "Have you had enough to eat yet?", they're terrified because they know there isn't anything left to give you if you said you were almost ready for another serving. After an awkward evening when the food ran out, you whined to your wife on the way home "Even though they're 2 of my best friends, I thought they knew me better. If they did, they would know they were just being unrealistic expecting me to just sit around after dinner for a long night of casual chit chat after they cruelly cut me off after my 3rd serving. They acted so offended, but what fat guy like me in the same situation wouldn't have ordered a pizza delivery to avoid embarrassing myself in front of everyone by passing out from hunger?"

You've learned to eat up on your 2nd and 3rd servings because you've noticed most hosts stop asking "Are you sure you've had enough to eat?" after that. For human land masses like you who are still looking for extra servings, that's when the host begins worrying it would be all their own stupid fault if they gave you an 8th serving. They know they would only have themselves to blame if they had to sit patiently with you afterwards till 3 a.m. making small talk until you finally had digested enough to fit back out the door.

When the host announces meekly "It's such a nice night, I thought we'd have dessert on the porch, if you don't mind.", you sense there's got to be a clever, ulterior motive involved considering it's 12 degrees outdoors and the snow is blowing sideways. Since they've tried this on you before, it can only mean one of two things. She either doesn't have enough food left to offer you a

6th serving or they've been doing secret circumference measurements as you ate and are confident you won't be able to fit back in after you scarf down the entire 3-layer cake.

When people wonder if you might stay for dinner they always say "Let me ask you what you will probably think is a really dumb question: have you eaten yet?" That's why no one is ever surprised when you respond "I ate about 15 minutes ago if that's what you're asking, but if you're wondering if I'm still hungry the answer is: 'Hell yeah!!!'".

When you RSVP, dinner hosts who know you well plan to feed 6 more people when you write '1 guest'.

It's always difficult for you to know how to respond to an invitation that requires an RSVP. When you go alone, you write '1 guest', but then the host always ends up being 2 seats short after you sit down. When you write '3 guests', the host gives a curious glance behind you wondering where the other guests are. As you're turning beet red with embarrassment, she displays her grace- ful etiquette by saying "Next time the custom that has evolved for Americans like you is to write '1 guest and 2 butt cheek creep chairs' so we have the right amount of place settings."

After 2 hours of continuously scarfing down plate after plate to the utter amazement of the host, you love to look around at the other dinner guests and say "Boy am I stuffed. I couldn't eat another bite." As they start to stare at you in disbelief, you say "Gotcha'! Just thought I'd lighten up the mood a little. Now, if you wouldn't mind, please start passing the leftovers and I mean 'all' of the leftovers this way."

With dripping sarcasm, after dinner sometimes you'll say "Gee, I can't believe there's nothing left to eat." whenever you secretly suspect your host might be withholding some food from you. At that moment, the room freezes when she tells you "As God is my witness, unless you want the cheese out of the mousetraps, you cleaned us out of every last crumb." There was such an awkward silence that ensued for a few minutes, which seemed like an eternity, you broke the mood by saying "Did you say there's cheese in your mousetraps?"

When you call an old friend and tell him "Heh, I was just in the old neighborhood and was thinking of stopping by...." and he and his wife meet you on the front lawn with a bagged lunch, don't feel insulted they feared you would eat them out of house and home if they invited you in. They just wanted to spare you the embarrassment of not being able to squeeze through the front door, after 5 kamikaze attempts, to make your way to their snack closet.

When you eat at the house of friends, they never have to ask anymore if you've had enough to eat because they know the doorbell will be ringing any moment after dinner from the Grubhub delivery guy if you didn't.

You've learned, without doubt, the best way to wear out your welcome as a guest. Once you see that the hosts can hardly conceal how annoyed they are about how long it took you to finish eating, you clink your fork on your wine glass and say "I have an announcement to make. Dinner was absolutely wonderful and this is why it's so terribly embarrassing for me to say, but I enjoyed the meal so much, I can't seem to get up out of my chair. Could I possibly trouble you for a bedpan, on the double?"

Whenever you're a dinner guest, you eat and eat and eat until one of the other guests can't take it anymore and rudely reminds you "You know this isn't an All U Can Eat diner, don't you?". You've heard this vitriol so often, you've learned to ignore offensive remarks about your gluttonous eating habits by deflecting and saying "I'm terribly sorry, I had no idea all of you were waiting for me to finish dinner… So, who's ready for some dessert?".

When neighbors invite you over, they take precautions for someone like you by hanging a 'No Hand Fishing' sign on their aquarium a 'Not For Human Consumption' sign on the dog's collar and a 'Please check between your butt cheeks for missing cat before you leave' sign on the couch.

When your waiter asks "Will there be anything else tonight or shall I bring your check?", you whisper to him "Psssstttt… heh buddy, this has never happened to me before, but I have an embarrassing request. I was just looking over the dessert menu for a can of WD-40 but it doesn't look like you offer it. Dinner was sooooo good, I'm going to need a few squirts on my love handles or else you're going to force me to walk out with one of your chairs stuck to my butt." After he gave you a strange look, he told you "You must not remember me. We don't list it on the menu, but give me a minute to look around the kitchen for the can we bought the last time you were here. If I can't find it, I'll put in a Grubhub order for a can from AutoZone."

When old friends call on New Year's Day and ask what you've been up to lately, you've learned to never use the expression "I don't get out much these days anymore." when you don't have much of a social life. Overly helpful friends always misinterpret what you mean and feel obligated to start giving you false encouragement by saying "Well, look on the bright side. Maybe with a lot less daily drive thru trips now, you might be able to fit out your door again by Springtime and at least get some fresh air."

When your closest friends give you birthday presents, they always warn "Be careful opening that. It might still be hot. I just took it out of the oven."

Instead of saying you just finished opening your presents for Christmas, you say you just finished eating all your presents.

On your birthday, you wish you had a nickel for every time your mom gives you a present and says "Don't wait too long to open it or it will be ice cold".

Your wife does all her gift shopping for you at drive thru's.

The people who know you best always show loving care to make sure your birthday presents are still warm when they give them to you.

Your wife is the one who's the last-minute Christmas shopper but she says it's because she likes to give you your presents while they're still warm from Grubhub.

As you're unwrapping the gifts people give you now, they always say "I can take it back if you don't like it, but why don't you taste if first. Now that I think of it, I'm not too sure if they even accept Christmas present returns at the McDonald's drive thru."

You've been accused of a lot of nasty things in your life, but at least you've retained some of your personal self-respect knowing no one would ever dare accuse you of being a picky eater.

All your Christmas presents come with microwave cooking instructions.

You put oven mitts on both hands before you open your Christmas presents.

When you're a houseguest and dinner is over and you get up to leave, the buddies who know you best silently get up with you and follow you to the front door. As you pause and they sense your indecision, they immediately call a goal line formation behind you. It never fails that even if they got no gain on the first 3 downs, somehow they always seem to be able to dig down deep and find the motivation to 'tush push' you out the door on 4th down and goal to go.

Whenever good friends ask nervously "Did you like your present?" when they obviously put a lot of thought into what to get you, you're always polite and say "It was absolutely delicious", even if you thought it needed more salt and was a little too spicy for your tastes.

The only curious comments you ever have about presents you receive from friends and family are "Hmmmm... this doesn't feel very warm at all. Ooooohhh, what a mystery gift! So… is it microwaveable or is it supposed to be served cold?"

You were so excited about your birthday this year, you ate all your presents before anyone could even sing happy birthday.

When you're a dinner guest, sometimes after an enormous dinner you'll say "Gee, I can't believe I ate everything already" as sarcastically as possible. You do this when you secretly believe your host is withholding food from you because she's worried that you're going to have to leave with one of her family heirloom dining set chairs stuck to your butt - again.

My wife hates how I embarrass her as I start scouting around the restaurant while I'm waiting for my order to come when we're supposed to be having a romantic evening. Dining out has become so expensive now though, it's the only way I can manage to get enough to eat. When you're respectful, you wouldn't believe how accommodating most patrons usually are when I say "Pardon me, I was just passing by on my way back from the men's room and happened to notice that it doesn't look like you're going to finish your meal. If you're getting a doggy bag, no problem. Forget we had this conversation. Otherwise, I'd be interested in making a cash offer for anything you're not going to eat. See that women over there who just covered her head with her jacket? That's my wife. When you're ready, just give me a signal and I'll take care of everything with the busboy."

When you're a dinner guest for the first time at a neighbor's home, you always have to remind yourself you're not at a buffet restaurant and have to pretend you have some social graces if you ever hope to be welcomed back. You were reminded of this once the gracious host had seen quite enough of your table manners. At the risk of embarrassing you and being known as a terrible hostess, she clinked her glass with a spoon and announced "Harvey, it's not polite to eat off of other guest's plates when they're in the bathroom. If it will help you behave, I'll have the leftovers scraped off of everyone's plate and give you a doggy bag before you leave....For everyone else, if there's something on your plate that you don't like, I'm not offended if you don't eat it, but please stop feeding Harvey under the table. One last thing. I hate to keep singling you out Harvey, but in a food fight, the proper etiquette is to throw food back at other guests, not try to catch everything in your mouth that's thrown at you... Now that I'm done with that unpleasant business, who would like a slice of pie?"

Exasperated dinner hosts often make a 'deal with the devil' with you when they're at their wit's end about how to get you to leave their dinner table. When she tells you "Listen, I'm going to give it to you straight: if you want another serving, I'm going to have to bring it out to you on the porch stairs. No offense, but, as your gracious host, I wouldn't be able to forgive myself if I gave you a

5th serving and that's the one that kept you from being able to squeeze your fat ass out the door." That's when you know you've got them right where you want them. At this pivotal moment, you're aware of something that she's not: no one has ever been dumb enough to invite you for dinner a second time. With this secret bargaining chip, you know if you agree to her last extra serving offer, you're going to be able to negotiate an unbelievably favorable deal on dessert terms.

Even when a host is completely disgusted by your revolting behavior at the dinner table, they've heard enough about you to fear letting it slip so that you would realize you're never getting invited back. Once a host makes the mistake of revealing that you've worn out your welcome, all bets are off with your pathetic attempt at having polite table manners. To get everyone's attention, you rip a huge fart, lay a Bic lighter down on the table and say "You can all wipe those fake, nervous smiles off your faces. Now that the jig is up, I'm going on record that those leftovers are getting wrapped up and put away over my dead body. If you all wouldn't mind getting back in your seats and sitting patiently for another 2 hours while I finish my meal, you'll never hear from me again. Now, nice and easy, if everyone can remain calm and start passing those bowls toward me, no one's gonna' get hurt. Trust me: that first fart was a warning. You do not want to see what happens if you make me ignite my next one."

14

WHY DON'T YOU GO AND PICK ON SOMEONE YOUR OWN SIZE... THAT IS, IF ONE EXISTS

WHENEVER I DON'T listen to my mom's old advice about waiting an hour after I've eaten before I go in the pool, I instantly regret my decision. That's because even if I wanted to go in for a quick dip to cool off I end up having to wait the hour anyway before I can digest enough to squeeze back out.

Neighbors wonder why I never cover my pool in the winter, so I usually tell them "I do it because you never know when you'll get an unseasonably warm day in the winter and wouldn't want to miss a chance to go for an off-season swim.", when the real reason is you have to bathe in secret in the pool now that you no longer fit in your tub.

A lot of moms have a rule for their kids that they can't swim until at least an hour after they've eaten or they'll get cramps. I was such a chubby kid, I didn't fit into too many pools, so my mom's rule for me was "Don't get dessert at Dairy Queen for at least an hour after you ate at Burger King or you'll get stomach cramps."

If you've been told once, you've been told a thousand times by your mom, when you bump into old friends, it's not polite to belly bump them into other zip codes when you greet them.

Parts of you that you've never seen before are already sitting down before you even decided to sit.

You've asked kind strangers as you're leaving highway restrooms if they wouldn't mind letting you know if you have a toilet lid stuck to your butt.

The only performance enhancing drug you're interested in is one that can help you chew faster so you can eat more on your 30-minute lunch break.

No one is ever surprised to see you when you tried to sneak up on them because they always recognize your man-made tremors minutes before.

You used to take selfies of your butt to post on-line, but had to stop because even Amazon doesn't sell a selfie stick that's longer than the 20 foot one you have that isn't long enough anymore.

When you bought a cemetery plot, they charged you with the same rate as an in-ground pool.

Whenever you horse around a little too much, you always know you'll be hearing soon from some whiny, world-renowned geologist who calls to scold you by saying "Now look what you've done!!! You cracked one of my best tectonic plates."

In the Springtime, people often mistakenly think you must be a former belly dancer, but it's actually because you're just trying to get your jiggling under control when you're sneezing all the time during allergy season.

You've reached that exceptionally rare level of obesity, achieved by very few, that is commonly distinguished by your face always looking like it's smooshed against glass now.

Your grandmother has been knitting you a sweater since she was a granddaughter.

You have trouble getting private time now because,
no matter how you try to squeeze it all in, some of you
always seems to still be in public.

When someone tells you you've got a great head on
your shoulders, you get embarrassed and then move a
chin flap out of the way and say "I know it's hard to spot,
but I actually do have a neck beneath my extra chins".

You used to put your wife on a pedestal when you got
married. For safety reasons, which you can never seem
to be able to find the right words to explain to her, you
eventually stopped because you began fearing she's got
to exceed the pedestal weight limit by a lot now.

Whenever you're around, people who know you well can
always tell you're nearby before they see you because
there's always an unusual increase in unexplained seismic
activity until you say "Hi guys! Sorry to sneak up on you."

The American Scientific Journal praised a world-
renowned astronomer for the discovery that all 400+
pound planetary-sized people follow a predictable, elliptical path on your orbit to and from the McDonald's drive
thru every 24 hours.

They say most people have a lesser chance of getting
hit by lightning than winning the lottery. You take up so

much more extra space now than most people though, your odds are about 50:50 now.

Your police file has BBQ sauce on your fingerprint records after the time you were arrested for aggravated assault on a buffet line.

You've learned to keep your pool only half full to avoid your 'tsunami effect' on unsuspecting neighbors when you do cannonballs.

Nothing could be further from the truth, but everyone seems to think you're a jolly fatso because every time you sneeze, they always start giggling while they're watching you try to stop jiggling.

You breathed a huge sigh of relief after your arrest when your lawyer got you freed by proving there was no law against defacing public property with man-made seismic activity.

You have to get new shocks, brakes and driver seat springs on your car every time you get your oil changed.

When you hear on the news that so many more people are living on the edge nowadays, you fear you may inadvertently be to blame because of all the extra space you're taking up.

The last time you tried to silently sneak by someone it still registered a 2.0 on the Richter scale.

When you tell people you're a self-made man, the thing that everyone thinks, but don't say is "This lard butt should've studied anatomy before becoming a self-made man. That explains though why he would have an ass in the front and in back".

When you were young and ambitious, you set out in life to put footprints in the sands of time. All you've managed to do so far though was crack a few tectonic plates.

When you get up to leave, other parts of you are still sitting down to stay.

Even when you're completely relaxed and having a great time, people are always telling you "You know you should really try to lighten up one of these days".

You always carry a can of WD40 to squirt on your belly when you're dining out in case the restaurant doorway looks like it's going to be a tight squeeze on the way out.

You've begun to hear a mysterious clapping sound behind you as you walk that eventually stops when you come to an abrupt stop, but only after what sounds like a 20 second standing ovation from your fat rolls.

You've effectively stopped gossipy people from being able to talk behind your back because there's really no telling where your stomach ends and where your back begins now.

You're surprisingly able to keep up with today's hectic schedules because you're one of those "unique in the history of humanity" overweight Americans who's gotten so humongous you can now be in two places at once.

You've unfairly taken the blame for a lot of unexplained public property damage, but you fervently protest that the San Andreas fault was not your fault.

You have been charged with a misdemeanor for a 2nd degree Conspiracy to Incite an Unscheduled Eclipse.

You asked your dermatologist if he was able to prescribe a 55-gallon anti-jiggle cream for the strange skin condition you have.

You've become such a talented cannonballer, you can jump in the pool blindfolded and still eject everyone who was in the pool back into the patio chair they were sitting in before they went swimming.

Friends have started asking you if you know any good fat jokes. When you look surprised, they apologize and tell you "I'm sorry, I didn't mean ones you came up with. I was thinking maybe you might remember some of the all-time great zingers people must have used on you before, you know what I'm saying?"

At Walmart, you're forced to wear a court-ordered sign on your back to avoid additional aggravated assault charges that says "If you can't see my elbows, I can't see what my butt is banging into on wide right turns".

Whenever there's been a tsunami anywhere in the world and the cause of it isn't known yet, you know it's only a matter of time before you get a knock on your door and get questioned by the police as a 'person of interest'.

You love having a pool, but you've just about had enough of nosey neighbors who are always asking "It's none of my business, but is it really worth it to have a pool if you have to refill it half way every time you go for a swim?"

You went on a canoe trip with your wife that was a complete disaster because you were so exhausted from doing all the paddling. In her defense, she told you "It's not my fault. I tried to help as best as I could but, no matter how far down I tried to reach, I couldn't get my paddle to touch the water the entire weekend.

You'd love to have a nickel for every time you've heard "Oh… It's only you. I thought I heard the rumble of thunder".

When you cannonball in your pool, neighbors wonder how your kids ended up in their pool.

There's no sense wearing a nice necklace when you go out anymore because it's too much of a bother to move your chins out of the way just to show it off to your friends.

You can't go to the beach anymore because of your restraining order that forbids you from getting closer than 1000 feet to any lake. You're still fighting mad about this because you think you were unjustly convicted of inciting a tsunami when the team of supposedly expert Geologists couldn't identify any plausible cause other than your cannonballs.

At weddings, everyone loves the new jiggle dance craze you've started, but when they ask you to teach them, they're disappointed when you tell them they would have to gain 300 pounds first.

You know you must be getting even fatter because you used to ask for help getting up from your chair, but now you have to ask for help pulling it off your ass.

On your criminal background check you have a misdemeanor charge for aggravated assault by using a cannonball to incite a tsunami.

You're always telling people "I just feel like a fat cow, but….do you want to hear something weird? It feels pretty darn good now that I've gotten used to lazily grazing all day."

The only way you ever surprise people is when they thought there wasn't a way in the world you could get any fatter than the last time they saw you 3 weeks ago.

You know you've gotten way too fat when at least 5 other areas of your body that are not your ass make spontaneous farting noises now whenever you stand up.

You've noticed you've developed this permanently funny smell that's no longer funny to anyone else who gets near you.

You're surprisingly able to keep up with today's hectic schedules better than most people you know because you've gotten so fat you can actually be in two places at once now.

Whenever a wise guy tries to trick you by telling you one of your shoes is untied, because he knows there's no way you can see it, you thank him and then bend over to tie it. As he starts snickering, that's when you blast him with such an epic, 1st degree, aggravated assault fart felony it's guaranteed to teach him, as he's gasping for air, to think twice next time about ever picking on a fat guy again.

People thought you were an underachiever in high school because they didn't give grades for your valedictorian performance in the cafeteria.

Of all your worst fears, you would rather be force fed a big bowl of Brussel sprouts now than to ever see yourself naked again.

When you're late for a meeting and tell your co-workers "I have to run", they always wait around for you to leave to see what you mean when you say that.

You feel like your lifelong best friends are becoming distant from you because no one ever tells you anymore "I'll be there to catch you when you fall" like they always used to.

You've gotten so fat, your mother scolds you "Honey, don't you remember when I taught you to do unto others as you would have done unto you? I know you think you can't help yourself because you've gotten so humongous, but it's not polite to smoosh people when you greet them."

If loveseats stick to your butt now when you stand up the way lawn chairs used to.

You can bump into old friends now that you haven't seen in forever and not even know you did it.

The Man-made global warming crowd is all confused now about what's to blame for rising sea levels and melting polar ice caps. It's all because they are starting to think the amount of methane gas being released in the atmosphere from the rapidly increasing group of American hippopotamic land masses is more responsible than the pollution from gas guzzling cars. Who knew, but the evidence clearly shows there are many more humongous guys like you around than there are of cars in America. Nothing could horrify the experts more. They're terrified the secret could get out, after all this time they've been telling everyone the problem is man-made, that it just might be the self-made men of the Golden Corral that have been causing it all along.

When you jump into the water at the beach at low tide and all of a sudden tsunami waves start flooding ocean front properties, even the global warming crowd would agree that it's likely there could be reasons other than melting glaciers that explain the rising sea levels in the United States.

People used to describe you as 'buff' when you were young and working out all the time. Now that you haven't exercised in years, they find it more appropriate to describe your mature shape as 'buffet'.

Your feet no longer get wet when it rains.

Whenever you were sad in your childhood because you were such a chubby kid, your mom would always try to encourage you by saying "Come on honey, things will get better soon. You've got to be more optimistic and try to keep your chins up."

You never spit anymore because no matter which direction you spit in now, it still lands on you somewhere.

I thought there was nothing my wife could do that could irritate me more than when she blew everything out of proportion all the time until she blew herself out of proportion.

Because you're so fat, you're limited to pairing up with a certain type of woman you try to pick up at closing time at your local bar. You'll know when you've found the one you've been looking for all your life when you can feel the tremors before you actually catch sight of her. When she seductively sidles up to you at the bar and says "Heh, big boy, whaddya' say we take this party back to my place? It's a double wide with a barn door, a king-sized bed and the refrigerator is full of Grubhub junk food leftovers.", you know she's the one. You've always dreamed about meeting a woman like this who you would like to spend all your time with, for the rest of your life, living happily ever after spending time together doing things that are fattening.

You wonder why when you tell people you want to be buried in the back yard they say "I didn't realize you had an Olympic sized swimming pool back there".

Whenever you sit now, part of you is usually accidentally trespassing in someone else's seat.

When you went on a whale watching cruise, you were so embarrassed when the whales watched you more than you watched them.

When you sit down now, your face cheeks get smooshed by your butt cheeks.

You think you figured out the likely reason why your friends didn't say anything, but must have unanimously decided they wouldn't carpool to work with you. After you had everyone over for a cookout, they had to have realized there wasn't a way in the world you could ever fit in any car with them when all of them couldn't even fit in your pool with you.

When you get out of your Olympic-sized swimming pool there isn't enough water left in there to go ankle wading.

When people who know you pretty well forget your name, they always get embarrassed and say something like "I'm so sorry, but I'm having a senior moment and can't remember your name right now. I can remember someone yelling out your name out at a county fair one time though. Is it SOOIE?"

It was a mystery to you when you started getting monthly membership junk mail asking you to join the American Sumo Wrestling Federation. All you could think was it must be just another one of those invasion of privacy secret satellite surveillance scams. They must assume I'd be interested simply because they spotted me on the beach in the only bathing suit that doesn't look completely ridiculous on me which is the Sumo diaper one I ordered on-line from a Walmart in Japan.

You're studying how semi-trailers take wide turns to learn how to keep your butt from causing any more merchandise damage claims when you take corners in stores.

You have to be careful what you order at restaurants now because some huge meals, which you absolutely love, you never order anymore because they have been known to turn your shirt buttons into deadly projectiles.

Thankfully you're oblivious to environmental whack job activists who look at you with utter disgust as you're eating a platter of greasy burgers from the Golden Corral buffet. They blame you so much for your reckless role in Global Warming, you're hated even more than dairy cows now for the amount of methane you must be emitting after a meal like that.

An astronomer demanded the right to rename you with a more planetary sounding name after he discovered you.

You always know someone is just trying to flatter you when they say "You scared me half to death! Don't ever sneak up on me like that again."

You're used to seeing stretch marks all over your body, but now you suspect you must be in your worst shape ever because you've never seen them before on your seat belt.

There are places beneath fat flaps on your belly that have seen less sun than the mysterious, giant deep-sea octopus.

When your doctor recommended you start taking daily walks for your health, he could see you had a strong aversion to taking daily strolls so he told you "You know, a lot of guys who are just like you don't like to walk either. They get used to it though by traveling in an elliptical path that will make the movement feel more like you're orbiting instead of walking, which should come natural for a guy like you who's the size of a small planet."

When people have a mistaken impression about what they assume is your cheery, optimistic outlook on life, you give a disgusted look and tell them "Listen: just because I'm fat and dumb, it doesn't mean I have to be happy".

Even though you became a successful businessman on your own, you never bother telling people you're a self-made man anymore. As a fat guy, you now agree it was just too much of a softball for any wise-ass not to pounce all over. Everyone would like some praise for their achievements, but it's not worth bragging about yourself when every time you did some snickering smart aleck would appear out of nowhere and say "I have a lot of admiration for the accomplishments of a guy like you who is completely self-made…… So tell me though, why is it that you designed a bigger ass in front than the one you have in the back?."

You were the inspiration for the EMT who invented the airbag when he came to your rescue after a rear end accident and helped pull your nose out of your bellybutton and noticed you didn't have a scratch on you.

When you're as fat as you are, it's easy to eat while you're driving on the highway because you've trained your belly to do all the steering.

When I went to buy my first package of Depends for drips and dribbles, I left the store in a panic after I discovered the largest size they make is Extra Large. Nothing has ever motivated me more to lose weight when I realized "Oh my God! If I don't lose 50 pounds – fast – I won't be able to be seen in public anymore unless I wear my cloth Sumo wrestler diapers." Not only would that embarrass me to no end, but the days of quick errands to the store would all be over. That's because there's no reliable way to tell the difference between an authentic Sumo wrestler and a regular Walmart shopper who is just wearing a Sumo cloth diaper while he's grocery shopping. Of course, the only way to find out who the real wrestlers are is an honor challenge for a belly bopping fight to the death. Try explaining this in the candy aisle when you're in your diaper and meet up with a real Sumo wrestler who wants to belly bump your ass into the parking lot when you just wanted to run a quick errand to re-supply on Snickers bars.

15

KING-SIZED MARRIAGES IN QUEEN-SIZED BEDS

WHEN OVERWEIGHT AMERICANS want to give a clear sign that they are committed to working on future growth in their marriage these days, they do it by getting a king-sized bed.

Your wife is so understanding with you, she even takes care of your every need when you're sleeping. Whenever you start moaning with pleasure as you're having an exotic dream, she'll sneak out of bed and tiptoe down the stairs to the kitchen. When she comes back, she puts a bib on you and a fork and knife in your hands to help you fantasize better about whatever it is that you're eating.

When you know the stresses of mothering have caused your wife to gain a substantial amount of extra pounds and dieting alone hasn't helped, it's never a good idea for you to politely suggest cardiovascular exercise. If by some miracle she agrees, I can almost guarantee she'll start by keeping her arms elevated over her shoulders to reach her training heart rate while she's throwing dishes at you for 15 minutes a day.

If there was a way to guarantee they'd lose weight by trying it, I'm guessing 9 out of 10 mothers who are unhappy with their weight would be willing to try the '90 days/ lose 40 lbs. Induced Coma Diet'.

It's become somewhat of a family tradition each year prior to our family beach vacation for me to give my sons the following warning: "If you don't want mommy to bash your iPhone to smithereens with a sledgehammer again, heed my words. You better believe her when she says not to take pictures of her at the beach in her bathing suit again until she's in good enough shape to have Sports Illustrated take the pictures for their annual bikini issue. Ignore me at your own peril, but know that Hell hath no fury like when a mom finds out a compromising picture in a bathing suit has been posted of her on Instagram or, even worse, on the cover of the grocery store tabloids playing frisbee in the waves with the Sasquatch."

When we first got married, my wife slept on the left side of our queen-sized bed. Once we started having kids, for some reason unknown to me she moved to the right side of the bed. Now that she's packed on her middle-aged, worried mother anxiety pounds she sleeps on both sides of the bed – at the same time. I can only speak for me, but I think this is the point for a husband, who has always disagreed before, to start thinking that the king-sized bed that she's been asking for throughout your marriage is starting to sound like a great idea.

Whenever your wife wants to go out for dinner, it's always an anxious, nail-biting time waiting for her to get dressed. The worst is when she can't find anything she would like to wear. You can't believe how much trouble you can get into when she just screamed "We're not going anywhere. I can't find a single thing that fits!" All you have to do is try to make even one helpful comment like "I think the Snuggie I bought you for Mother's Day is still in the clothes donation bag. Would you want to try that on to see if it fits or should I order pizza?" and your days of going out to eat are o-v-e-r.

When my wife comes out of the bathroom now after weighing herself for her diet, it reminds me of back in the day when I would wait on pins and needles for her to come out with the results of her pregnancy test to see if a celebration was in order. I have the same silent, anxious anticipation, but now I hope against hope to hear the wonderful news "You can stop fidgeting. We can finally celebrate. I only gained 3 pounds on my diet this month."

When you feel like you've tried everything you can possibly imagine and truly have no idea anymore how to make your impossible husband happy, try losing 40 pounds to see if that works.

When your wife has been struggling with her weight for years and has become completely frustrated when she tells you "I've tried every diet and none of them work. I haven't lost an ounce no matter what I do. It must just be my metabolism.", simply nod in agreement and keep your big, fat mouth shut. No matter how helpful you think your advice could be, at a difficult time like this it's never appreciated when you point out the obvious fact that she probably has to stick with the diet for more than 6 hours to start seeing any visible results.

Developing good instincts matters if you ever hope to survive as a husband. It's like when you have an unhappy overweight wife and you're shocked to discover a smashed scale in the bathroom one day. At a moment like this when your extreme curiosity is making you wonder "What in the world could have possessed her to do something like this?" husbands who make it for the long haul understand some concerns in marriage are better left as unresolved mysteries.

I was shocked about the romantic response my wife gave me the one and only time I was dumb enough to mention the diet she was on. She told me "You are my forever love, the man of my dreams, the answer to my prayers, my one and only and I adore you and cherish every moment I've had with you, and yet.... if you're ever dumb enough to give me dieting advice again, there won't be any warning shots next time."

When you first got married, you vowed to stick with your wife through thick and thin. You're still committed to your marriage, but to avoid sounding completely ridiculous at your 25th anniversary renewal of your vows, you made a new pledge to stay loyal to her through thick and thicker.

When you argue with your mature figured wife now, as a safety precaution, you secretly clutch a red cape behind you in case she charges.

Your wife tells everyone she knows that we have a 'fairy tale' marriage. You don't agree with her because you secretly think there's no way she could ever be considered the beautiful damsel in distress in a fairy tale anymore. You don't know what she's been reading, but, when the desperate call goes out for her hero prince to rescue her in the formulaic fairy tale, you have never heard of the brave prince having to save her by removing the lawn chair that's stuck to her butt just before the fire breathing dragon arrives.

When she looks at you like you're an idiot for asking what she likes to do in her free time now, I know she's thinking "Duhhhh… it's not obvious that I like to do things that are fattening?"

You and your wife have gotten so big it's like a subconscious, supine, sumo wrestling match when you both enter your queen-sized bed each night to see who gets the bed and who gets belly bumped out and has to sleep on the floor.

Way back when we were having our kids, I remember my wife was always on my case about reading the book 'What to Expect While She's Expecting' so I could understand what she was going through. Despite all her pleading, I mainly used the book as a beer coaster to her everlasting disgust. Now, 20 years later, the tables have turned and the situation seemed ripe for payback. For Christmas this year, I bought her a book called 'What to Expect When It Looks Like He's Expecting'. Her response was far from the empathy I expected for a loved one in my fragile condition. I'd share her reaction if I wasn't such a fraidy cat about doing that. All I'll say is I know for certain now that empathy lives on a One-Way Street in marriage.

Whenever my wife loses a significant amount of weight on a diet, I secretly start hiding her fat clothes before she can stuff them in the clothes donation box so they'll be ready and waiting when she'll need them again 3 months from now.

You point at different body flaps now while you're yelling at the kids and say "You see this? That's one of the horrifying prices I paid for being a good mother!".

When you boast to people that it was "love at first sight" for you, they assume - as impossible as it seems – that somehow you must not have seen her butt first.

After your 10th anniversary, you agreed to add a secret vow to your original marriage vows that you will never – ever – initiate an unplanned discussion about your wife's weight again. In the event you do, you've already signed a 'hold harmless' legal agreement concerning bodily harm that says "Due to husband-induced tempo-rary insanity, she's not responsible for whatever happens next, but you can be sure it won't be good."

When you asked your husband why he never introduces you as "my better half" anymore, he said "Don't get me wrong, I would love to honey. I just hate whenever I say this in front of people who it turns out know a lot more than me about fractions and they start laughing at me like they wonder how I could have ever graduated from 6th grade math class."

You're secretly amused that your wife always blames the dog when she can tell someone's been rifling through the kitchen trash can.

You used to let your wife handcuff you to the bed to add some excitement to your sex life. You finally put a stop to it when you realized she only does it now to deprive you of being able to get out of bed for your midnight snack.

You and your wife share the same worst fear now: ever seeing each other naked again with the lights on.

Your wife hates keeping leftovers that end up as one of your midnight snacks, but she ends up keeping them anyway because it's like a lesser of two evils for her. She's noticed that whenever she keeps them, at least you seem to eat out of the trash less.

When your wife asked you to do driver training with your 16-year-old son after he got his driver's permit, the only driver training he got from you was circling drive thru lanes of all the fast food places in town whenever you weren't ordering or picking up your food.

Your wife would love to lose some unwanted weight too but has trouble dieting because she can't overcome the psychological barrier that it might look like she's hard up enough to try and please a blob like you.

When your wife complains you have nothing in common anymore after 20 years of marriage, you gently chide her by saying "Don't be ridiculous honey. Isn't it obvious we both love doing things that are fattening?"

Your wife has gotten so big over the years, whenever she whines now "I can't find a single thing in the closet that fits me", you tell her "Well duhhh… if it fit you now, how in the world is it ever going to fit in the closet?".

Now that you've gotten so fat, you practically have to beg your wife to help you with taking a bath now on Saturday nights. She hates getting out the fire hose, broom and 55-gallon drum of liquid soap, but the worst thing is having nosey neighbors taking Tik Tok videos while she's scrubbing you in the pool. She's gotten so fed up with doing this, even though she knows it's one of my favorite things, she told me "Listen tubbo, it's embarrassing enough to have to bathe you in the pool, from now on bubble baths and rubber duckies are off limits until you can fit back in the tub."

Your wife thinks you have insomnia when you're tossing and turning in your sleep, but it's actually just paranoia about oversleeping and missing breakfast.

When you tell people it was love at first sight when you met your wife, they assume it must have been a panoramic view.

As your marriage matured and grew, you had to go from a Queen-sized bed to a King-sized bed to a Kingdom sized bed.

Foreplay for you now involves trying to remain calm as you're staring at your wife while she knows she's teasing you and driving you wild with such desire you don't think you'll be able to take another second of waiting just as she yells "Dinner's ready!!!"

When your middle-aged wife tells you she's so excited that she can finally wear a bikini again, you do your best to pretend you share her excitement when you tell her "That's just wonderful honey. I'm so happy for you!", but secretly think "Lord help me! If she's planning on wearing it in public, I hope it's only as a wrist band."

When your wife points you out at a social gathering to let someone know you're her husband, she asked if you'd prefer her to describe you as the humongous one or the hippopotamic one over there stuffing his fat face with appetizers. It's so insulting to you that she would ask your preference when you already told her at the last party you attended together that humongous is clearly the more respectable description.

Your wife always knows when you've had a great dream because you always keep her up for half the night while you're chewing in your sleep.

When you wake up and notice your wife's face looks as flat as a pancake, you've heard it so many times before you don't even have to guess what happens next. The moment she takes one look in the mirror, she starts whining "I can't believe you squashed my head again. It's going to take half the morning for it to get back to its normal shape. We're going to have to get a king-sized bed if you can't keep your belly from making frisky border intrusions on my side of the bed after I fall asleep."

There are less family pictures of your wife at the beach than the National Enquirer has of the Sasquatch.

Even though your wife has warned you over and over again that you could cause a serious accident one day, you still plop into bed sometimes when she's sleeping because you think it's so cool how you can make her levitate above the bed for a couple of seconds like you're Obi Wan Kenobi.

Even though you've both gained a ton of weight since you got married, after all these years your wife still knows how to drive you wild in the bedroom. At this point in our 30-year relationship, nothing inflames me more with desire on a Saturday night than when my wife walks into the bedroom in a sexy nightgown and places a plate of brownies on the bed. After winking at me with a seductive, knowing look, she says "You better let those sit for a minute, Lover Boy. I just took them out of the oven.". After that, she takes off her nightgown and goes to sleep in the guest room.

You used to have hungry eyes for your wife. Nowadays, she can only rekindle that old, desperate, horny look when she holds a bag of Doritos next to her face.

When you're new to marriage, you hear your wife say a lot of things that sound perfectly reasonable at first that later make you wonder if you've always been this naïve. Take the first time she was donating clothes for example. When you asked a question about the clothes that looked brand new, she told you "I'm giving these away because they're my 'old' jeans, honey. They fit when I was younger, but I couldn't fit a leg in them now." At first, you accepted what sounded like a perfectly logical response. After you look at the receipt though, which she forgot she left in the pocket, you discover how the 'old jeans' classification actually works for a wife. It's basically determined by the number of wears or age. 'Old jeans' are anything that have been worn twice and no longer fit or are 90 days or older and aren't even worth trying on now because it would be a miracle if they still fit.

When you were young and horny, your wife definitely knew what you wanted on a Saturday night. Now that you're old and fat, she's not so sure. She came to this conclusion when she told you seductively one Saturday night "I know what you want, big boy". After hearing this, you went and put your bib on, grabbed a fork, knife and a beer and then sat at the kitchen table waiting for your surprise, while she was waiting in bed in her new negligee wondering where you were.

I talk in my sleep, so my wife will selfishly ruin my best dreams sometimes just so she can have a peaceful sleep by telling me "I'm sorry sir, but we're all out jelly dough-nuts. If you can wait till tomorrow night's dream, we should be completely re-stocked by then. Thank you for your continued patience. Good night."

You have a number of different foreplay techniques that used to work like a charm to get your wife in the mood when you first got married. None of these can even get her to budge off the couch anymore though. Thankfully, you discovered a new method that has a fantastic rate of success to entice her to follow you into the bedroom. You could just kick yourself now it's so obvious, but all you have to do is carry around a box of a dozen warm Krispy Kreme donuts you just took out of the microwave and she'll follow you just about anywhere.

You used to start foreplay with some passionate necking but now the only thing that gets her going is French Fry kissing.

Your wife studies Kharma Sutra sex positions, but it's only to see if they have any good recommendations on methods to avoid suffocation and asphyxiation.

You bring your wife's favorite cupcakes to bed when you're in the mood to help her with her fake orgasms.

You haven't said anything, but it annoys you to no end that your wife falls asleep right after sex because you have no idea it's from suffocation.

On Saturday nights, when you tell your wife "Ooohhh baby, you know the words I want to hear", she tells you "To be honest, it's been so long I feel like I used to know, but I'm not exactly sure I do anymore. Are they 'Be careful; I just took that out of the oven?"'.

You think your wife might be part native Indian because a local tribe in your area calls her Heap Big Woman.

When your wife tells you she's excited that she can finally wear a bikini again, you know it would be too dangerous to utter any type of response at the time, but you've become gravely concerned that this can only mean one thing: she's slowly going blind!

When your wife told you "I'm planning on getting rid of a lot of unwanted weight soon", you were excited at first until you realized that might just be her subtle way of letting you know you should keep a bag packed for an upcoming mysterious disappearance.

You can always tell when a mother hates how she looks in family pictures. You'll find more pictures in the family photo albums of sasquatches poking their heads out from behind trees on a camping trip than you'll find of her. To her, vacation pictures from the kid years are all classified as Top Secret, Weight Watcher 'Before' pictures that no one will ever see until she declassifies them with ones she can contrast with 'After' pictures that haven't been doctored.

My wife and I both love the beach, but I'm really hesitant to go now that we've both gained a lot of weight, yet she still insists on wearing a bikini that looks ridiculous on her. Of course there was no way humanly possible to tell her this. That's why I decided my best option would be to use reverse psychology. I said nothing, but bought a skimpy bathing suit of my own, intending to make her be too embarrassed to be seen at the beach with me. My plan was so successful, all eyes were on me for once. I eventually had to stop parading around in it though because you can't believe how much of your boxer underwear can get bunched up in the butt crack of a teeny bathing suit. It was so bad, by the end of a day playing in the sand and frolicking in the waves it looked like I had a Depends pantload in my Speedo. Even though this did distract all of the attention away from my wife, she didn't seem to mind at all and even posted my picture on Instagram. I've decided to go back to my old, baggy bathing suit now because I'm sick and tired hearing from old friends and family that my beach pantload pic just reached 10 million views.

Just because I'm fat, my wife acts like she thinks she's my mother sometimes and will make rules I had as a kid like "Don't swim until at least an hour after you eat or you'll get cramps and die". Thankfully, it's as easy now as it was then to find loopholes in her totalitarian rules. The other day she yelled to me when I was in the pool, "There's a delivery guy in the driveway who says he has a delivery to a pool…. Did you order pizza?" so I admitted it was for me. Then she wants to know, "Why in the world would you order a pizza delivered to a pool, of all places?" At times like these you know a wife hates to be accused of sounding like she's stupid. What other option is available though when the truth was "duhhh…I was really hot and wanted to go for a swim, but I was also hungry. This was the only way I could figure out how to do both without violating your 'Wait 1 hour after eating' pool rule."

My wife was pissed about how much weight I gained during the COVID quarantine, but it wasn't because of how bad I looked. Her problem was that I got so big I didn't fit into our shower anymore. As a result, I needed her to help when I needed a bath by scrubbing me with a broom in the yard and spraying the soap off with a hose. It was fun for both of us at first, but I agreed with what she said about this not being a laughing matter anymore on really cold, winter days. While she was freezing cold in her rain suit and rubber boots, I always tried not to laugh while she was miserable, but it always tickled me into giggling whenever she scrubbed my armpits. She would get so mad, anytime I made the slightest request like "Would it be too much to ask for more peanuts while you scrub?", I would get the vitriol of "Listen lard ass, one more word out of you and you can go find your own freakin' circus the next time you need a bath."

As a husband, a painful lesson I've learned is women react differently than guys do when you deliver a great zinger about being out of shape. It doesn't matter how hard you've worked to establish a loving and supportive persona; you never earn a free pass to fire off a fat one-liner that is so good you just can't help yourself. Just wait to see what happens next if you caught her at a vulnerable moment when she needed her understanding husband, not the wise-ass one. Sometimes your puny brain betrays you though and allows you to say stuff like "Honey? I know you're dejected and you've told me it's something I could never understand. If you don't mind my saying so though, to me there's no sense wondering if any of the clothes in your closet fit anymore if you can barely squeeze into the closet to try them on." If you're ever dumb enough to do this, the only good thing that will come of it is the instant cure you'll provide to her fragile state of mind. She's guaranteed to immediately forget about her frustration with trying on clothes that don't fit and, in her blood-curdling rage, start thinking about where she left her gun.

You feel like an idiot calling the contractor who did some remodeling for you 3 months ago to make a complaint about his work. Just to appease your wife though, you call him and say " Don't get me wrong: we think the work you did on the master bedroom closet looks amazing and the quality is top notch, but we've both noticed a disturbing flaw since you finished......She has no idea how it's happening, but my wife swears that all of her clothes have been shrinking ever since you completed the job last winter......Weird, huhh? I think it's probably got to have something to do with the type of wood you used. Have you ever heard of this happening before? If so, what would you recommend?" In short, he had been informed of this phenomenon by many customers who have wives who weren't happy with their weight. The only way he'd discovered to avoid the problem was to stop renovating master bedroom closets in the winter.

When your wife buys clothes that are too big for your sons, she always tells them "Don't worry, I'm sure you'll eventually grow into them." and it always turns out that she was right. When a normal American husband sees this, he'll get this brilliant idea in his puny male mind "Hmmmm… That's some impressive, cost-conscious thinking. Maybe I should recommend doing that with her clothes." If you do, you might - might - get the benefit of the doubt the first time you follow this theory with some clothes presents you bought for your wife, but don't count on living to tell the story a second time. It's not as if she didn't grow into them just as you predicted she would. Your dilemma is you just hadn't learned yet that sometimes when you're right in marriage you couldn't be more wrong in the big scheme of things, especially about any brilliant suggestions you think you've had that involve her weight.

If you've never heard steak knives whizzing past your ears and thunking menacingly into a wall or felt the terror of having the cold steel of a pistol barrel against your neck - and have a morbid curiosity what this would be like - you should try getting married to a woman who is never happy about her weight. When I'm busy pushing my wife's buttons, I've never had such a clear under-standing of when I'm risking "crossing into a no man's land of no return" as I say something like "The problem, as I see it, with all the diets you've been on before that didn't work is you've got to give them more than 3 days to work before you start smashing the bathroom scale with a sledgehammer again. Now if you were to ask me, which - for the record - I'll acknowledge you haven't, I would tell you.......What, huhhh?!? Not this again. Why is it that every time I try to have a serious talk with you about your health you ask me to wait a second while you run and get your gun?"

My wife complained to her nutritionist so much about not losing any pounds on his weight loss plan, he had to remind her that she was supposed to include a regular exercise plan if she wanted to reach her weight loss goals. A month later, after she told him she'd been exercising regularly for the last month and didn't lose an ounce, she accused him of being a fraud and fired him. From what I'd seen, the only cardiovascular exercise I'd seen my wife doing was smashing our bathroom scales into smithereens with a sledge hammer a few times a week whenever it provided a number she obviously wasn't happy with. Naturally, that's why I had to swear on our first born that I wholeheartedly agreed with her about him being a fraud when she said "What does any guy know anyway about a woman's preferences for exercise?"

You end up having a lot of ridiculous discussions when you're married, like the times when your wife is stuck and needs your help. This type of conversation always begins when you hear her yell "Help, I'm stuck! Can you come and get me out of here?". You get a little alarmed when you hear this and immediately go to find her, only to be baffled when you get there and ask in disbelief "Stuck?!? How in the world did you get yourself in there in the first place?" At this point of the story, a lot of unmarried people would say "Aren't you being a little hard on her? What's so unusual about that? Lots of people have discussions about needing help when they're stuck somewhere." When you tell them "In the bedroom closet though, after we'd already talked many times before about the real risk of this happening when you're binge eating cookies while trying on pants that don't fit?", that's when they agree that type of conversation is probably limited to the 'Overweight American Married Class.'

After packing on extra pounds every year of our marriage, my wife was ecstatic when I finally got serious about dieting and lost a lot of weight. A woman in this situation vows "Never again will I wear my fat clothes!" and goes out and buys a completely new wardrobe. My wife had no idea that guys never part with their favorite high school clothes and was shocked when I dragged them out of the attic and didn't have to spend a dime on new clothes. Now that I'm walking down memory lane again in my polyester, bell bottom pants, silk shirts with ruffles, neon-green tank tops and velour tracksuits, she looks at me like she wishes she had been more careful what she wished for. Without saying a word, I think she prefers the old me back or at least a version that doesn't embarrass her in public more than I did when I was a blob. I mean why else would she begin counting my daily calories again based on the FDA's recommended daily allowances and strictly limit my portions to those of a family of 6?

Whenever your wife wants to go out for dinner, it's always an anxious, nail-biting time for you to wait around downstairs - between now and forever - while she's getting dressed in the bedroom. Even if you're half-starved waiting for her to come down the stairs to announce she's finally ready, you're expected to be a good husband and patiently wait for her announcement. For this predicament, I always thought the worst-case scenario was when she screamed "We're not going anywhere. I just tried on everything in the freakin' closet and can't find a single thing that fits!" It turns out there's something worse – much worse. From experience, you know the odds are stacked against you for going out when you've been waiting for more than an hour. At that point, the slippery slope you face is deciding when to call for a pizza delivery so you can eat at a reasonable time without your wife discovering you have no faith in her to find something that fit. That's why if you screw up the timing, when you just heard the announcement that you're not going out, it's not helpful if the doorbell rings just as she finished her sentence and then asks "I wonder who that could be?"

16

THE USUAL REPORTS OF UNUSUAL REPORTS OF SEISMIC ACTIVITY WHENEVER YOU'RE AROUND

IF YOU'RE A bully, but agreed to follow the advice your dad gave you of "If you want to fight, next time pick on someone your own size.", you'll only be discouraged to learn how difficult it is to find someone your actual size when you weigh over 400 pounds. To make things even more difficult, when you're all excited that you finally found someone your size and start to pick on him, he tells you "Whoa, whoa, whoa pal, wait just one, hot minute. If you're challenging me to a fight, the only way I'll agree to fight you is if you're properly attired. My dad always told me "If you want to go around picking fights, never disgrace our ancient honor code of Sumo wrestling by ever fighting anyone who isn't wearing a cloth diaper."

You told Weight Watcher's you were quitting because it was just making you too exhausted and hungry trying to watch all of your weight at the same time.

Lately, you've grown very attached to what you used to tell people was the unwanted weight you were trying to lose.

The only way you ever surprise old, high school friends anymore is when you arrive at the next class reunion and they suddenly have a déjà vu moment about thinking the exact same thought they had at the last reunion. As you greet everyone, you can almost mouth the words as they shriek "Oh my God! Same old Harvey. I didn't think there was any freakin' way you could get any fatter than when I saw you last time. Good for you, old pal. You've always been able to prove everyone wrong when you set your mind to it."

You're always telling people "I just feel like a fat cow nowadays.....You want to know what though? It's starting to feel pretty darn good now that I'm getting used to it."

You try to hide at all costs that you've noticed whenever your wife has put on a ton of weight. That's why you turn off the lights and hold on as tight as you can to the bedpost before she plops into bed so you don't embar-rass her by getting catapulted out of bed and posterized against the ceiling again.

Weight Watchers has to chart your progress on a Richter scale because the one they got from the zoo to weigh the elephants didn't go high enough.

Stepping on bathroom scales now leads to a new level of cursing even road rage drivers, bad golfers and minivan moms would be envious of.

Even after 5 years as a dues paying member, receptionists still welcome you every time you visit Weight Watchers and take a 'Before' picture before they show you where the snack machines are.

When you haven't seen old friends in a while, they always ask you if you've lost weight because they know you're always on whatever the latest fad diet is at the time. When you answer "'I haven't weighed myself recently, but, unfortunately, I don't think I have.' they tell you, 'Yeh…It didn't look like you had but we figured you would be expecting us to ask and we didn't want to disappoint you by not noticing that you hadn't."'

When you're on the doctor's office scale for your annual physical, the disgusted nurse told you your weight reading would be more accurate if you could show some willpower for a few seconds and put your bucket of Kentucky Fried Chicken down for a moment.

When you bump into old friends and they ask "What's new?" and you tell them "Well… the big news is I recently lost a lot of weight.", they always gulp reflexively and then stare at you with a stone-faced look of disbelief. When they finally stammer "I…I…I…I'm so sorry, I would have said something if I'd noticed, but I… uhhh… am at a loss for words.", you tell them "Well duhhh… Once I realized what I'd done, I was so terrified about how to act in this virgin territory of being trim and healthy I gained it back as quickly as I possibly could when I feared it might be lost forever".

You've started bragging to everyone you know "I've reached the point where I can stuff me face all day now and never gain an ounce anymore.", but anyone you tell this to immediately thinks "Duhhh, the only way you could be naïve enough to think that is if your scale only goes up to 375 moron."

You get so suspicious about what the ulterior motive must be of any old friends who are always broke when they tell you "Wow! You look great… have you lost a lot of weight?" Whenever someone tells you this, you usually reply "I'm really sorry, but I can't help you out right now. With a ridiculous compliment like that, it sounds like you could use a few bucks on loan, but I'm flat broke right."

You know you must be getting too fat when people ask if you've gained weight since the last time they saw you and that was at breakfast.

If Jesus had caught sight of you in the crowd just before he was about to pull off the "loaves and fishes" miracle, he would have had to revise his dinner plans and say "This has been great, but - wooo, look at the time - it's getting late so whaddya' say we break for supper and meet back here around 7?"

Your bathroom scale fears telling your wife her actual weight more than the Wicked Witch of the West's mirror did of telling her who's the fairest of them all.

When you finally resolved to get back in shape, but didn't think you were ready yet to adhere to the strict discipline required to join Weight Watchers, you joined the Whale Watchers program instead.

You've never been one to worry too much about seating capacity at restaurants. Once you're seated though, you do start to get increasingly worried about your seat's capacity the longer you've been eating.

You're so heavy now it's useless to use a bathroom scale anymore to find out your current weight, so you had to go out and buy a Richter scale.

When you think back on it now, there must have been clear signs when you were younger that you would have weight problems later in life. Whenever you were really worried about something back in those days, your parents always encouraged you, but they'd do it by saying something like "Whatever it is you're worried about, it can't be that bad, honey. C'mon now son, keep your double chin up. We know you. If you just try your best, you'll find out there isn't a single problem in life that you can't eat your way out of."

Co-workers weren't sure what to say to you on this sensitive subject so they all got together and decided to congratulate you on your apparent weight loss when they noticed the catsup stains on your shirt were much lower than where they normally saw them.

You know you've gained weight but have no idea what you weigh now because your scale only goes up to 375. Surprisingly, this has helped you regain a level of self-respect whenever you meet someone new and they tell you "Hoooweeee...... You are one ginormous porker. You must weigh a ton!" and you reply "Actually I weighed myself just this morning and, believe it or not, I'm still only 375."

When you drive your 1-ton truck everyone thinks it must be a 2-ton truck.

You're sure you must have gained a lot of weight over the holiday season, but thankfully can't be sure exactly how much. That's because, no matter how you maneuver yourself now, you still can't see around your belly anymore to see the number on the scale.

You play your new, all-time highest weight in the daily pick 4 lottery each week now.

Even though you're still worried about your weight, you stopped weighing yourself all the time because of the huge hassle it is for you to get this done. You're sick of the long drive, having to pay admission each visit and then having to stand in a long line every time with the elephants at the zoo just to find out what you could have already guessed that you gained even more weight.

When you've struggled with weight problems your whole life, you learn to hate when you meet up with old friends you haven't seen in a while. That's because you could just about barf when they start showering you with false praise about how good you supposedly look. It never fails that they compliment you by saying "We had trouble finding you in the crowd because we were looking for someone who we thought would look much heavier by now. You look fantastic! You couldn't have gained any more than 20 pounds since we saw you a couple of months ago. What's your secret?"

One of the things you hate the most about being fat is how old acquaintances make pathetic attempts to be polite when you eventually meet up again and never fail to ask you if you have lost weight. When you tell them "No, I don't think so. If anything, I might have even gained a few pounds since the last time I saw you", they say "Yeh, that's what we thought. It didn't look like you had but we figured we'd be polite and ask anyway just in case you'd be disappointed if we didn't, considering you've been on a diet for the last 20 years."

At your 'never seen before in human history' level of obesity, you could just about puke nowadays whenever your supposed best friends try to commiserate with you about your weight. They just sound so insincere when they say stuff like "This might sound awkward, but I'm not happy with my current weight either. I could defi-nitely stand to lose a few pounds myself, so I know what you're going through. Somehow though, you make me feel like everything is okay with my extra weight when I reflect on how much worse it could be when I look at you. I guess what I'm struggling to say is thank you from the bottom of my heart for not only always being there for me, but for always being so big it feels more like an entire crowd has my back."

You're skeptical that your bathroom scale can give an accurate weight reading anymore because you assume correctly that it can't be counting all your pounds when you're on the scale while part of your belly and butt is resting on the floor.

It's getting close to critical mass with your weight if you've had to glue a mirror onto your old 10-foot selfie stick because it's the only way now that you can see what the reading is on your bathroom scale.

You were in great shape and had an amazing figure in high school so they nicknamed you Buffy. Now that you're out of shape and on your 6th figure since graduation, all your old schoolmates pronounce your nickname as 'Buffet' now.

After she saw your results, your wife practically feinted when your medical report showed that you hadn't gained any weight since your last annual physical. What you failed to mention though is the old scale in the doctor's office only goes up to 375 pounds.

You've become so self-conscious about your weight, whenever anyone gives you an accusing look, you completely panic now and instantly blurt out some ridiculous plea about your innocence like "I know what you're thinking, but I didn't have anything to do with it, I swear. You've got to believe me! I've never even been to California so there's just no way the San Andreas fault could have been my fault." You can always tell when you've overreacted when they tell you "Take it easy, pal. I was just going to tell you got barbecue sauce all over your cheeks at lunch."

One of the things you learn as a husband to promote peace and harmony is to never comment on your undeniable observations of alarming weight gain on your wife. You'll learn heaping helpings of holidays followed by months of layers in shapeless clothing in winter seclusion promise Spring surprises some years that require you to summon all your powers of blind idiocy to pretend not to notice. I was too terrified to mention it this Spring, but of all the record setting weight gain years she'd had previously, what I was absolutely convinced was my wife's worst winter weight gain disaster ever surprisingly turned out to be our new baby boy Fred.

People can tell you're not too sensitive about your record setting weight gain over the winter when you wonder with excitement what size the clothes manufacturers will describe you as next.

You blamed your wife for your drastic, sudden weight gain because she failed to mention she bought a new bathroom scale that goes up to 350 when the old one only had a 300-pound max.

There's never a weight capacity warning listed on folding chairs, so you're always throwing caution to the wind whenever you dare to sit in one. When you take a chance at a cookout, there's a hushed silence from everyone there to see what happens next. If the chair goes 'splat' immediately, they'll know it wasn't designed to support all of your 350 pounds. If it doesn't collapse, everyone

knows that when you decide to go back for a third helping in about 20 minutes, you're going to need help
pulling the lawn chair off your butt.

People know you either lost or gained weight when they
hear you coming because your flubber flaps are making a
different clapping sound lately.

Your next-door neighbor says she can always tell if she
has gained weight over the winter when she tries on
jeans she wore last year the next Spring and they don't
fit. You tell her you know exactly how she feels when you
open your pool in the Spring and the first time you try to
go for a swim you don't fit.

When old friends haven't seen you in a while, they know
to look for someone who looks like you but is probably 10 pounds heavier by now. That's why you chuckle
the next time you make plans with them to meet at a
restaurant. When you see them looking right at you
and they still don't recognize you, it's because you've
gained 20 pounds since the last time they saw you 4
weeks ago at Thanksgiving.

After you've had lunch, sometimes you enjoy the time
alone just sitting on a mall bench and relaxing while
you digest. It never fails though that you eventually get
furious and stomp off in a rage, when complete strangers won't mind their own business and keep stopping by
to ask "Heh buddy, sorry to bug you, but is this where

the Weight Watcher's 'Before' models are auditioning? I don't want to be rude, but if you're auditioning, I guess I might as well go home instead of wasting my time."

You point your thumbs at yourself and always give a sarcastic look when you say "Duhhh" to people when the elevator door opens and they ask if you're going up or down.

You can only take elevators down now, no matter which buttons you press.

You get a secret thrill from the fear you see in the eyes of co-workers as they get on the elevator with you on the way back from lunch. Whenever the elevator stalls between floors, you know you have the absolute power to incite an all-out panic anytime you feel like it by simply saying "I don't want to alarm any of you, but does anyone happen to have any Beano?"

When the elevator door opens and the person standing there gets a puzzled look and asks "Going up?" and you say "yes", they usually give you a second glance and then step back and tell you "Fat chance".

You have to admit it's a petty pleasure, but all the same you love to see the desperation in your fellow passengers' eyes when they frantically review the maximum weight capacity data plate when you step on the elevator.

You try your best not to stare at people in elevators whenever you're stuck between floors. Even though you hope the thought would never cross your mind, you know anyone who gives you a terrified look is probably thinking that you're deciding who you'll eat first if you're stuck for more than an hour.

It's so embarrassing for you whenever you're stuck on an elevator for more than 15 minutes. All the other people stuffed in with you start giving you frightened looks when you try to sneak an embarrassed glance at them. That's because your assumption is correct that they're thinking "I wonder who he's going to eat first if this ordeal goes on for very much longer" and you're so embarrassed because that's exactly what you were thinking.

You've gotten so heavy, you're paranoid now about reading weight limit signs everywhere you go to avoid a catastrophic accident. It's gotten so bad, you even stop before old, rickety bridges now that have signs that say 'Weight Limit 1 Ton' to do a few quick calculations to see if you should re-route your nav.

You've gotten so heavy lately, when you plan long drives now you always use the 18-wheeler truck driver 'weight restriction avoidance' routes just to be cautious.

For any man to ever achieve his lofty goal of truly understanding a woman he must understand how any woman, who in all other matters seems to have a clear and logical thought process, is capable of making an accusation that the most despicable, rassa frassin, cold-hearted, ruthless liar she's ever known is her current bathroom scale.

You don't have to count on an unreliable groundhog's prediction to know when the first signs of Spring have come when you're married. Beginning in late March, all you have to do is sneak stealthily into the hallway and simply put an ear up to the bathroom door and listen quietly each day after your wife just walked in there. Once you hear "Oh my God! What have I done?!? It's only 3 months until I've got to squeeze these extra 20 pounds of winter weight into my new bikini for our summer vacation!!!", you'll know she'll soon announce her first gimmicky diet plan of the year. This is always the first sign of Spring in my house. The 2nd sign is she won't look in her mirror again until she can see her shadow in a bikini and doesn't feel the need to hide out for 6 more weeks.

Of all the things you have to be concerned about when you're super fat, skinny wiseguys are the worst. They're always lying in wait for the right moment to catch you off guard by asking innocently "Have you lost weight recently?" If you're secretly thrilled by this compliment and then dumb enough to fall into the trap by saying "Thank you for noticing. As a matter of fact, I have lost a few pounds. To be honest, I didn't think anyone would be able to tell.", that's when they drop the bomb. You only have yourself to blame when everyone starts yucking it up when he says "If you were concerned about where you might have lost them, you can stop your worrying. I know you can't see what I'm seeing, but I'm staring in disbelief at your butt right now and somehow they got packed right back here on your ass."

Your wife complains to you that you must not be as attracted to her as much anymore because you always used to put her on a pedestal as a girlfriend, but never do now that she's your wife. Nothing could be further from the truth, but I'm sure a lot of understanding husbands who've experienced this dilemma would agree with me that there's no way to explain your reasoning without making things even worse. I mean how in the world can you have a rational conversation with your wife when the only possible explanation is "No offense, honey, but you couldn't be more wrong. You're still a sex goddess to me, but I felt compelled to stop for your own safety. I admit I don't know what the exact limit is, but I began to fear, especially after you became a wife and then a mother, that you've got to be way over the pedestal maximum capacity by now."

One very important way marriage is unlike a circus is you definitely don't get a prize when you guess the fat lady's weight. This is confusing for any man because, when your wife was your girlfriend, she never minded letting you guess how much she weighed and proudly told you her actual weight afterwards. Something strange and frightening changes though after you get married and have kids. At some point, guessing her weight is not a game anymore and becomes more like an Iron Curtain state secret that will only be divulged under penalty of death. Take my word for it that this is not a subject to casually bring up in a conversation because you're mildly curious about it. If you doubt me, try even once to start dancing around the topic with your wife and she's guaranteed to tell you "So you want to play our old circus freak show game about guessing the fat lady's weight, huhhh??? Is that what you're up to dipshit? Well, I'd like to introduce a new circus game of my own instead that's fun for the whole family. Go get me a blindfold, an apple and all my steak knives and I'm going to show you how the crowd favorite 'The Spinning Wheel of Death' game is played!!!"

Normal sized people have no understanding why you hate to go to reunions now that you've gained a ton of weight since college. The reason is no one recognizes you anymore as you get teary-eyed when you first see your old friends and go to hug them and see abject fear in their eyes instead. It's so obvious that they're thinking "Who is this terrifying fat guy who looks like he's about to smoosh me like I'm his middle seat mate on the plane?" It never fails that your best old buddies you haven't seen in ages look at you, do a double take, then look at your name tag, then look at you, then do another double take, then look at your name tag, until you finally interrupt and say "Fred, do you really mean you don't recognize me? We were roommates for 3 years and I was the best man at your wedding. For heaven's sake it's only our 5th year reunion."

Whenever you see someone come into the elevator after you, they try not to be rude but, as you see them start to look panicked, you know enough to step aside because they need to face their fears and take a glance at the weight capacity plate. Somehow this gives them peace of mind that they can determine if they're in for a slow ride to their floor or if they should start praying fervently because they'll likely be plummeting down the elevator shaft soon toward their untimely death.

www.ingramcontent.com/pod-product-compliance
Lightning Source LLC
Chambersburg PA
CBHW071925150726
47999CB00001B/102